EGYPT

A JOURNEY THROUGH THE LAND OF THE PHARAOHS

Conducted by James Henry Breasted, Ph.D.

Professor of Egyptology and Oriental History in the University of Chicago
Director of Haskell Oriental Museum of the University of Chicago
Director of the Egyptian Expedition of the University of Chicago

With the Stereographs of

Underwood & Underwood

CAMERA/GRAPHIC PRESS LTD.
NEW YORK

© 1978 Camera/Graphic Press Ltd.

This new Camera/Graphic edition first published in 1979 is an abridged republication of the first edition published in 1905. This edition was entitled *Egypt Through the Stereoscope* and appeared as a single volume accompanied by a boxed set of 100 stereographs. A new preface has been added.

Library of Congress Catalogue Card Number 78-65711

ISBN 0-918696-11-9

Cover and Book design by Hermann Strohbach, New York.

Production by Irwin Wolf, New York

Printed in the United States of America

CAMERA/GRAPHIC PRESS LTD.
P.O. Box 1702, F.D.R. Station
New York, N.Y. 10022

CONTENTS

JAMES HENRY BREASTED

James Henry Breasted was born in Rockford, Illinois on August 27, 1865. After studying theology for two years, Breasted found the countries of the Bible so fascinating that he abandoned a church career for Egyptology and archeological research. He joined the University of Chicago faculty in 1894. In 1901 he became director of the Haskell Oriental Museum a position he held until 1931.

He mounted his first major expedition to the Near East in 1905 when he lead a large group of American scientists of the University of Chicago. Both an Orientalist and historian, Dr. Breasted would become synonymous with archological exploration and discovery. He viewed the "Rise of man from savagery to civilization as the most remarkable phenomenon in the history of the Universe as we know it."

The Megitto Expedition of the University of Chicago which he headed in 1928 discovered the site of Armageddon and a great number of Hittite relics and skeletons.

His translation of a remarkably erudite medical work written about 1700 B.C. on a fifteen foot scroll of papyrus was considered a landmark in the history of medicine. He published the translation and commentary under the title "The Edwin Smith Surgical Papyrus."

Due to Dr. Breasted's intimate association with Howard Carter and Lord Carnarvon and his work in the Tutenkhamon tomb, unusually heavy emphasis was placed by the attending physicians at Dr. Breasted's death (Dec. 2, 1935) on the post mortem substantiation of the diagnosis in an obvious desire to eliminate any possibility that Dr. Breasted's death might be attributed to the widely circulated story of the "curse" of Tutenkhamon. Dr. Breasted himself once described the so called curse as "tommy rot."

PREFACE

At the turn of the century, when this statement was made, the stereoscope was indeed a source of entertainment and education in many homes. Delightful hours were passed with its wonders, one of which was the "travel-at-home" series of stereographs published by the firm of Underwood and Underwood, enabling those who had little or no hope of ever visiting the strange and fascinating places portrayed by its photographers to make an imaginary journey to those foreign shores themselves. Published in sets, with an accompanying book often containing maps and illustrations, they transported the viewer to the exotic lands of Europe and the Far East on a conducted tour guided by a leading authority of the day.

The stereoscope, the marvelous instrument that made all this possible, was invented by an English physicist named Wheatstone who first announced and demonstrated his stereoscope in 1838, just a year prior to the announcements of the discovery of photography by Daguerre and Fox Talbot. With the advent of photography the preparation of photographic prints suitable for stereoscopic examination followed.

The stereoscopic camera employed two lenses which were placed about 2½ inches apart on the same level, this distance equaling the average distance between the human eyes from center to center. It is, in effect, a double camera producing a 3-D effect.

The publishing of stereographs, the photographs produced by this camera, started one of the most fascinating forms of entertainment in the Victorian Era. It was to the Victorians what television and movies are to us. Millions were entertained and instructed on a variety of subjects — travel, history, religion and art, among others.

Stereoscope views were first introduced commercially into America by the Langenheim Brothers of Philadelphia in 1850. By 1880, the stereo craze started to die down until Bert and Elmer Underwood, two young brothers, entered the field, starting what was to be one of America's most successful publishing companies. Opening their business in Ottawa, Kansas in 1882, primarily as agents for other stereo companies, they grew rapidly through door-to-door selling and a sophisticated mail order and advertising campaign. By 1891 they had begun to publish their own stereo views and had relocated their head office to New York City.

At this time Bert Underwood, having been in business for ten years and never having picked up a camera, took up photography himself. The result was his travel series on Greece, Italy, and the Holy Land published as sets. By 1901 the company was manufacturing 25,000 stereo views a day and 300,000 stereoscopes annually. In 1896 Elmer and Bert took a photographic tour of Egypt where Bert made the negatives that are now reproduced as stereo views in this book. "Egypt Through the Stereoscope," the first publication of these photographs, consisted of 100 views, a book and a set of maps. Each view bore a caption in six languages — English, German, Spanish, French, Russian and Swedish — and a printed excerpt from the book on its back. As was to be their practice with the some

300 sets they would publish during the years 1902-1910, the Underwoods engaged a prominent authority to write the guide book to accompany the views.

James Henry Breasted, one of America's foremost Oriental scholars, was Professor of Egyptology and Oriental History in the University of Chicago from 1894 through 1925, Director of the Haskell Oriental Museum and Director of the Egyptian Expedition of the University of Chicago, 1905-1907. His own introduction, chronological table and description of each view comprise the text of this new version of the original book. This renowned and respected scholar, steeped in the 6,000 year history of Egypt, writes for the armchair traveler who, with little or no knowledge of that wonderful civilization, wished only, with the aid of a stereoscope, to be entertained and gently educated. Professor Breasted succeeds admirably, conducting his tour with verve and enthusiasm. It is rather startling to remember that we are in the year 1905 as he discusses the excavations and discoveries being made, to realize that the great treasures of Tutankhamun were not to be found for almost twenty years hence and sad to read of his dread for the fate of the beautiful island of Philae, "doomed to destruction" by the threatened construction of yet another Aswan dam, an event already planned but not to occur for another sixty years. He mourns lyrically for the romantic, gentle isle "set like a peerless gem among the wild, desolate rocks of the cataract, still softened and enriched by the swaying palms. . .what will become of this beautiful island?" As we look at the photographs of Philae, as it was, we understand his anguish, for though her monuments have been saved, her lovely island is lost forever beneath the waters of Lake Nasser.

With few exceptions, though, Egypt has changed little in the time since Professor Breasted conducted his tour. His words remain as informative and interesting as they were then, the stereographs as beautiful, bringing to life the history and art of the greatest civilization on earth.

Beryl A. Veasey, editor

6

INTRODUCTION

The University of Chicago
April 1, 1905

In connection with the duties of university teaching and its modern obligation to carry on constant research, it has also been my privilege, during the last ten years, to begin the work of making a public wider than that of the university lecture room acquainted with the life, customs, history, and monuments of the ancient Egyptians. In this latter attempt I have met with a number of different plans for private study, for class study, for lecture courses and the like, among women's clubs, extension centers, literary societies, and similar organizations. I have been and am still constantly appealed to for outline studies and lists of books, which will furnish the individual student and the reading class or study-circle with the material necessary for their study. Heretofore, I have never been able to find any books or material which could furnish graphic reproductions of the remains still surviving in the ancient lands of the East, or of those lands and their people as they are today, coupled with an adequate account of their long history, their life and customs.

It was, therefore, with peculiar satisfaction that I made the acquaintance of this system of stay-at-home travel, the great merits of which are but beginning to be appreciated. By its use an acquaintance can be gained, here at home, with the wonders of the Nile Valley, which is quite comparable with that obtained by traveling there. In my judgment there is no other existent means by which this result can be accomplished. These superb stereographs furnish the traveler, while sitting in his own room, a vivid prospect as through an open window, looking out upon scene after scene, from 100 carefully selected points of view along the Nile. By this means then, the joys of travel can be extended to that large class of our people who thirst for an acquaintance with the distant lands of other ages but are prevented from doing so by the expense involved, or by the responsibilities of home, business or profession.

It was with this conviction that I have undertaken, in the midst of numerous other duties, the task of standing with the traveler at every point of view, to be his cicerone, and to furnish him with the indispensable wealth of associations, historical incident, or archaeological detail suggested by the prospect spread out before him. Nowhere in the ancient world have its great monuments been preserved in such numbers, or so completely, as in the Nile Valley, and nowhere, therefore, is the visitor carried back into the remote past so vividly as among the myriad monuments that rise along the shores of the Nile. Realizing, then, that this land of monumental marvels, so rich in the works of men, has in the past been closed to the average man and accessible only to him whose means and leisure permitted him to make the journey of the Nile, I have here endeavored to work out this system of travel for Egypt. It enables the great host of those whose constant dream of travel has heretofore remained unrealized to stand under the shadow of the greatest architectural and other monumental works of the ancient Orient and to feel with the sense of substantial reality that these venerable structures are actually rising yonder before the beholder's eye. These experiences in the presence of all the myriad witnesses of a mighty past can not only be a source of untold pleasure and instruction, but also can enormously expand the horizon of daily life, more truly making the beholder a "citizen of the world" than he can ever hope to be without actually visiting these distant lands.

In the preparation of the following pages, I have constantly had my eyes within the hood of the stereoscope, and I cannot forbear to express here the growing surprise and delight with which I observed, as the work proceeded, that it became more and more easy to speak of the prospect revealed in the instrument as one actually spread out before me. The surprising depth and atmosphere with which the scientifically constructed instrument interpreted what were actually but bits of paper and pasteboard, were a revelation; indeed, I constantly sat by an open window looking out over the actual ruins of the Nile Valley, which I could study, one after another, at will. To the believing beholder there are precious moments when the mind is perfectly convinced of the reality of the scene before him, and such moments, persistently sought and repeated, come more and more easily as one accustoms himself to the instrument, until, afterward, the mind looks back upon it all with essentially all the sensations of having seen the reality; an actual visit to the place can do little more. Moreover, by the repeated use of the stereograph, the scene can be often reimpressed upon the mind's eye, and herein lies one of the greatest advantages of this system of stay-at-home travel, that the trip may be made as often as one likes.

The selection of the places to be visited and studied by this system has not been an easy task and another, familiar with the country and its monuments, might have made a different choice in some cases. The number of considerations involved in making a representative selection is not small, and every effort has been put forth to be fair to all these considerations.

Should this book fall into the hands of an oriental scholar, let him be assured that the orthography of the Arabic proper names is as unsatisfying to the author as to him. It should, however, be remembered that this book is intended for practical purposes, in the hands of readers who know nothing about and care less for the intricacies of Arabic orthography, readers to whom the complications of a full and correct system of transliteration, however carefully explained, would mean nothing and cause only vexation and confusion. In the reproduction of such names, the simplest possible form has been used, with practically no diacritical marks. If the reader unfamiliar with Arabic will pronounce all the vowels as in Italian, or the continental languages, they will be nearly enough correct for his purposes. The necessity of maintaining the sense of location is sufficient reason for the colloquial tone adopted in these rambles. This will also explain the insistent repetition of the bearings and orientation of each position, a repetition which experience has shown to be essential and useful.

James Henry Breasted

THE STORY OF EGYPT

There is no people whose career can be followed through so long a period as that of the people of Egypt. The civilization of Babylon may be older though that question is still under debate, but Babylonia so early disappeared as a nation that the length of its career is shorter by many centuries than that of Egypt. Egypt still survives with a people of the same mental characteristics and the same physical peculiarities as we find in those subjects of the Pharaohs who built the pyramids. They have changed their language once and their religion twice but they are still Egyptians as of old, pursuing the same arts, following the same occupations, holding the same superstitions, living in the same houses, using the same medicines, and employing the same devices for irrigation and cultivation of the fields which the student of the monuments finds among their ancestors 5,000 years ago. The amazing persistence of the chief elements of their civilization, the survival of these things into our own times, is due in large measure, if not solely, to the very unusual natural conditions under which they lived. We must therefore note briefly the geography and climate of the Nile valley, if we would at all understand the marvelous people who so early found a home there.

The whole northern end of the African continent is traversed from the Atlantic on the west to the Red Sea on the east by a vast desert which is continued eastward through Arabia and far into the heart of Asia. This desert of two continents is crossed by two great river valleys: in Africa by that of the Nile; in Asia by the Euphrates valley supplemented by that of the Tigris. These two great river valleys, one in Africa, the other in Asia, formed the home of two remarkable peoples to whom the classic world of Europe and through it we ourselves, owe the fundamentals of civilization which were there developed from the most primitive beginnings to a high degree of perfection and then transmitted to the European nations in the basin of the Mediterranean. He who would know the story of man, and particularly its first chapter, will find it necessary to delve long and patiently among the surviving remains in these two river valleys, for *there* is the earliest human culture which we are able to date with approximate accuracy, as compared with the vast range of uncertainty in the date of the remains of early man found elsewhere by the anthropologist, like the relics of the cave-dwellers of prehistoric Europe. We are to journey together through one of these ancient cradles of civilization and I repeat, we must know before we enter upon the journey, something about the valley, its climate and the other natural conditions among which its people lived.

Rising at a point three degrees south of the equator, the Nile flows northward through equatorial Africa until, 1,500 miles after passing the lakes called Victoria and Albert Nyanza, it is joined from the east by a great affluent coming out of Abyssinia. From the color of the water the western river is known as the White Nile while the eastern is called the Blue Nile. After their junction the common stream is the Nile proper. The territory thus far traversed by the river is a vast and fertile region known as the Sudan which means "blacks" and refers, of course, to the race inhabiting the region. At the junction of the two Niles is the frontier town of Khartum; about 140 miles north of this place the Nile receives another tributary from the east, the Atbara, which is its last affluent; on all its long journey to the sea it receives no further contribution to its waters but must make its way through the desert alone. For just below its junction with the Atbara the Nile enters the table land of Nubian sandstone which there underlies the Sahara; for over 1,000 miles the river must fight its way through the tough sandstone which forms its bed and not the countless ages which have elapsed since it first debouched upon the Sahara have sufficed to wear away a perfect channel.

In many places the huge and stubborn rocks are piled in masses in the stream, dividing the waters into numerous, tortuous channels where they descend with rush and roar, only to meet with similar obstructions below. These are the so-called cataracts of the Nile which break the stream at ten or more points; but they fall into six main groups, so that it is usually stated that the cataracts of the Nile are six in number. They are not what we generally understand by the term cataract as there is no sudden and great fall as in our cataract at Niagara. Finally the river escapes from the last obstruction, an outcropping of granite which thrusts up its rough shoulder at Assuan where the stream emerges upon an unobstructed course of some 700 miles to the sea. The reason for this difference is that the bed of the Sahara, at a point about 65 miles below Assuan, suddenly changes to limestone, a less refractory material through which the river has worn a wide, deep channel. Something over 100 miles before reaching the sea, the river divides into two branches, the western, called the Rosetta mouth and the eastern, known as the Damietta mouth; but in antiquity there were seven such Delta mouths of the river. From the source to the mouth it is about 4,000 miles in length and thus ranks with the longest rivers in the world. The Delta was, of course, originally a large bay which has been gradually filled by silting up from the river.

The valley of the Nile is simply a vast canyon cut across the eastern end of the Sahara from south to north by the age-long erosion of the river. This canyon in the long, dreary stretch of the sandstone country above Assuan is shallow and narrow, so much so that it can in places hardly be termed a canyon; but below Assuan, where the limestone begins, the canyon is 14 to 32 miles wide and the cliffs or bluffs on either side are frequently several hundred feet high. Flanking these cliffs are the desert wastes, less barren and forbidding on the east. We shall often take our stand upon the crest of these cliffs and overlook the valley, so that we need not further describe them here. Egypt proper extended from the sea only to Assuan, or the first cataract, as the *last* cataract obstructing the river is usually called because it is the first one met in the ascent. Egypt was and is, therefore, a vast trench in the Sahara to which we must add the Delta, the scattered oases in the desert on the west, the eastern desert to the Red Sea, with the greater part of the Peninsula of Sinai. Of cultivable soil the narrow valley above the Delta contains less than 5,000 square miles, the Delta itself somewhat more than that, so that the entire area of habitable country is under 10,000 square miles. Within such narrow limits as these, about equal to the area of Vermont and Rhode Island combined, developed the remarkable civilization which we are to study. It will be seen that we have here natural boundaries producing unusual isolation; on the north, the almost harborless coast of the Delta; on the east and west the desert, and on the south the cataracts. Here, the earliest Egyptians lived in the greatest security and seclusion and under such conditions have not only developed but also preserved many striking and individual characteristics.

The climate, although not absolutely rainless as often stated, was and is effectually so as far as agriculture is concerned. The people were thus forced to depend upon the annual inundation from the river for the fertilization of their lands as well as their irrigation after the waters receded. Of all this we shall see many examples when we have entered the country and we shall not wonder that the people early developed mechanical arts when forced to the daily use of clever devices for the utilization of the river, whether in irrigation or navigation. They enjoyed a climate which was, to be sure, intensely hot in summer, but in winter equable and delightful to a degree that is now drawing thousands of convalescents to Egypt every season. Here, then, recent excavations enable us to trace the prehistoric Egyptian, in the fifth or possible the sixth millennium before Christ, as he passes from the use of stone and pottery to the conquest of metals, the acquisition of writing and an ordered civilization under a king.

The earliest Egyptians were probable related to the Libyans and at some remote period of their history they were invaded by tribes of Semites, as in the 7th century A.D. the Arabs came in and made conquest of the country, at the beginning of the spread of Islam. This prehistoric invasion brought Semitic elements into the language and gave it a fundamentally Semitic structure. Doubtless, also, some things hitherto unknown there were imported into the material culture of the earliest Nile dwellers. The resulting composite race, of African-Libyan and Semitic-Asiatic origin, is that which emerges into the light of history in the middle of the 43rd century B.C. when they had already sufficient knowledge of astronomy to introduce a calendar with a year of 365 days. This is the earliest fixed date in history (4241 B.C.).

We dimly see at this remote period, two kingdoms on the Nile; one in the south, occupying the valley proper; the other in the north, that is, the Delta. These two kingdoms of Upper and Lower Egypt were united some centuries later into one nation under one king and thus Egypt, as a homogeneous nation, is born. Menes, the king under whom this union was accomplished, thus heads the long list of dynasties and the line of Pharaohs begins. This is called the dynastic period because from now on we find successive generations or families of kings called, as in European histories, dynasties, as numbered and enumerated by the Egyptian historian, Manetho, who wrote in the middle of the 3rd century B.C. The chronology of these dynasties is in the greatest confusion, but it is probable that the accession of Menes and the beginning of the dynastic age falls not later that 3400 B.C. although it may possibly be 100 years earlier. Beginning here, then, we look down the changing panorama of Egyptian history during nearly 5,400 years to the present. Of this vast sweep of years, only the first 2,400 or 2,500 were under native Pharaohs, for since the middle of the 10th century B.C. Egypt has been under foreign kings with but trifling exceptions. We see her then under her native kings, making the earliest chapter in human history of which we are adequately informed. The first two dynasties of kings, living on the upper river, near Abydos, were masters of a civilization from which we have, with slight exceptions, only material remains; but these are of such a character as to arouse the greatest admiration at the technical skill of these remote craftsmen on the one hand and their fine sense of beauty on the other. But we cannot trace the political career of these earliest dynasties.

The Old Kingdom
2980-2445 B.C.

With the accession of the 3rd dynasty we are able to discern something of the political conditions as we see Egypt rising into her first great period of power and prosperity which we call the Old Kingdom. It includes dynasties 3, 4, 5 and 6 and lasted from the early decades of the 30th century to about 2400 B.C., nearly 600 years. It offers the oldest example of a developed civilization that is in any adequate measure known to us. Even granting that Mesopotamian culture is older, it presents for the period of the Old Kingdom only an isolated date or two with here and there a royal name. But to the existence of the kings of the Old Kingdom their pyramids still bear vivid witness; and often, too, these royal tombs are surrounded by a silent city of mastabas (masonry tombs), the walls of whose chapels acquaint us not merely with the names but in graphic bas relief also with the occupations, pastimes and daily life of whole generations of grandees who formed the court of the Pharaoh in life and in death now sleep beside him. Hewn in granite, limestone or diorite, their faces are familiar to us and even the flesh and blood features of one of these antique Pharaohs of the Old Kingdom have survived to look into our faces across nearly fifty centuries.

In order to view the career of the kings of this period we must station ourselves at the southern apex of the Delta, on the western side of the river where the ruins of Memphis lie, for their royal residence was always in or near this city. Here we might have seen the Pharaoh ruling in absolute power, sending his officials from end to end of his kingdom and dominating a functionary-state, the officials of which lived at court directly under the monarch's eyes. It was therefore a closely centralized state, the power of which was focused in the person of the Pharaoh. Had we walked the streets of Memphis we would have found three classes of people at least: at the top and bottom, the noble and official governing class, and the serf; but it is impossible to think that the magnificent works of the Old Kingdom in art and mechanics, many of which were never later surpassed, could have been produced without a class of free craftsmen. There was, therefore, a free middle class of artisans and tradesmen. Art in sculpture and the crafts attained a marvelous perfection; literature flourished; and in religion appear traces of an ethical test applied to every one.

It is far easier to draw a picture of the *life* of the Old Kingdom than to trace its *history*. Purely monumental materials are often eloquent witnesses of power and splendor but give us little of that succession of conditions and events which form history. Imagine an attempt to trace the history of Greece solely from its surviving monuments; much of the temper of the Greek people may have found expression there but little of the course of events which marked their political history and still less of the gradual mental unfolding by which a people of rare intellectual powers developed with unparalleled rapidity from childish myths to the profoundest philosophy. So in the 4th dynasty its rapid rise is evident from the enormous size of the Gizeh pyramids, but of the other deeds of their builders we know little. Already in the 1st dynasty the Pharaohs had begun mining operations among the copper veins in the Peninsula of Sinai and left their monuments of victory there. Snofru, the last king of the 3rd dynasty, continued these enterprises and sent fleets on the Mediterranean as far north as the slopes of Lebanon where they procured cedar for Snofru's buildings. After three-quarters of a century of ever-increasing power and splendor, the 3rd dynasty was then succeeded by another family, the builders of the great pyramids of Gizeh, the 4th dynasty. The possibly three centuries or more during which the 4th and 5th dynasties ruled clearly show a steady decline in power after the first century, if the decreasing size of the pyramids is any criterion; until in the 6th dynasty it is evident that the central power is slowly disintegrating. The Pharaoh's governors in the local administrative districts had gradually gained hereditary hold upon their offices and the districts they governed. They thus developed into a class of powerful landed lords and princes. They no longer build their tombs alongside that of the Pharaoh, but are buried on their own ancestral estates where they have doubtless resided rather than at court as before. They were gradually drawing away from the king who was unable to prevent them from attaining a greater degree of independence.

A court favorite of the time, named Una, has left us in his biography an account of how he led a body of troops into the Peninsula of Sinai, where he five times routed the Bedouin enemy. After this he brought his army by sea on an expedition, as he says, "north of the land of the sand-dwellers," that is, the Bedouin of Sinai. North of them means toward if not into Palestine, as he speaks of reaching certain "highlands" which may be those of Judea; but few details further than the defeat of the enemy are given. Already at this remote age, the noblemen of the Pharaoh carried on for him traffic with the east African coast near the mouth of the Red Sea, the region which we now call the Somali coast. These are the earliest voyages in the open sea known in history. On the southern frontier similar officials carried on caravan trade with the Sudan and subdued the warlike Nubian tribes in order to keep open the southern traderoutes. We shall visit the tombs of these aggressive nobles at the first cataract. There are also evidences of trade with the Agean islands in the Old Kingdom.

Having ruled some 150 years, the 6th dynasty sank gradually into obscurity; with it fell the Old Kingdom, leaving as its witnesses the irregular line of pyramids which stretch from Abu Roash, opposite the southern apex of the Delta, southward for 16 miles along the margin of the desert to Sakkara beside the ruins of ancient Memphis.

With the overthrow of the Old Kingdom we see the seat of power gradually moving up the river from Memphis. The local barons who have now gained their independence, are contending among themselves for the crown. Of the 7th and 8th dynasties we know nothing but we shall see in our voyage up the river the tombs of the nobles of Assiut, the vassals of the 9th and 10th dynasty kings who ended Memphite supremacy and lived at Heracleopolis.

The Middle Kingdom
2160-1788 B.C.

The Heracleopolitans were unable to maintain themselves against the nobles of the south, especially the princes of Thebes, a city which at this point, for the first time, appears among the contestants, in so far as we know. You will find it at an important strategic point upon the river, not far above the bend, where it approaches most closely to the Red Sea (south of its northern arm, known as the Gulf of Suez). Thebes from now on plays a prominent part in the history of the country; for a Theban family of nobles succeeds in pushing down the river, overthrowing the Heracelopolitans and setting up a new dynasty, the 11th. This begins Egypt's second great period of power which we will call the Middle Kingdom. As the 11th dynasty was succeeded by the 12th, also of Theban origin, the power of Thebes was firmly established over the whole country and thus about 2000 B.C. the country entered upon two centuries of unexampled prosperity and splendor. The organization of the new government was essentially that of a feudal state, a fact which shows that during the obscure period that preceded, the nobles have won a large degree of independence the beginnings of which we have already seen in the 6th dynasty. Social conditions have not materially changed since the Old Kingdom.

In order better to govern their new kindgom the powerful monarchs of the 12th dynasty, the Theban Amenemhets and the Sesostrises, moved down the river to a point not far from the pyramids of the Old Kingdom, probably just above Memphis and there they ruled with a sagacity and firmness that kept their family on the throne for over 200 years. This is the classic period of Egyptian history; the system of writing for the first time attains a consistent and fixed orthography and literature flourishes as never before. The arts continued to develop with unprecedented splendor, medicine and elementary science made great progress; in religion the ethical element had now triumphed and the ethical quality of a man's life determined his destiny hereafter. The resources of the country were developed and utilized as at no time before. The kings executed enormous hydraulic works for recovering a portion of the flooded Fayum, a large oasis on the west of the Nile valley, so close to it that at some probably prehistoric period it was flooded from the inundation by the river forming the Lake Moeris of Greek times. Near the same place Amenemhet III built the vast structure known in classic days as the labyrinth. Aboard, Sesostris III followed up the campaigns of his ancestors in Nubia so successfully that he conquered all the territory above the first cataract as far as the second and made his permanent frontier at a point above the second cataract where he established several strong fortresses to maintain it, thus adding 200 miles of Nile valley to the kingdom of Egypt. This province he then connected with Egypt by a canal at the first cataract. Trade with the southern Red Sea countries was still maintained. We hear even of a campaign in Syria, though its results were evidently not lasting. Traffic with the Aegean islands was not uncommon. Thus the Middle Kingdom, the feudal age of Egypt, shows itself more aggressive both at home and abroad than the Old Kingdom, the age of the pyramid builders.

The 12th dynasty kings have also left us their pyramids extending in a straggling line from Dashur, just south of Sakkara, to Illahun, in the mouth of the Fayum. Of their temples next to

nothing has survived owing to the complete rebuilding under the Empire. Under their successors of the 13th Dynasty, the power of the Pharaohs is again on the decline, resulting finally in the second period of uncertainty, like that which followed the Old Kingdom. Passing over the obscurities of the period, all that we certainly know is that for a few generations before its close we find the country in the power of foreigners, usually called the Hyksos (after Josephus), who took possession of the Delta and the valley for an uncertain distance up the river. They came from the north — that is, Asia — and were probably Semites.

The Empire
1580-1150 B.C.

Against these usurpers the Theban princes, the successors of the Middle Kingdom Pharaohs, finally waged a war of independence which was brought to a successful issue by Ahmosis, the founder and first king of the 18th dynasty. He drove the enemy from their stronghold, Avaris in the Delta, whence they fled to Palestine and there Ahmosis besieged them for six years in the southern Palestinian city of Sharuhen, mentioned also in the Old Testament (Joshua xix, 6). After he had expelled them and pursued them to Phoenicia, he returned to Egypt to wield a power up to that time unknown to any Pharaoh. For in the war for liberty and long-continued internecine conflicts the local barons have been practically exterminated and thus about 1580 B.C. Egypt begins her third period of power, which we may call the Empire, with a totally different organization from any that we have thus far found. It is now a military state, largely made so by the wars with the Hyksos who taught the Egyptians warfare and for the first time introduced the horse into the Nile valley. What few nobles have survived are no longer local proprietors, but simply hold rank in the

Pharaoh's service; the Pharaoh personally owns the land. For the first time there is a great standing army into which we see Egyptian gentlemen entering as professional soldiers, and from now on the soldier is the most prominent figure in political life. Side by side with him, and for the first time also a power in the state, now stands the priest. Soldier and priest, therefore, replace the barons of the Middle and the functionaries of the Old Kingdom.

From Thebes, now just beginning its career of splendor, the great military monarchs of the 18th dynasty went forth to cross the isthmus of Suez and conquer Palestine and Syria, or to pass up the river into Nubia and push the frontier of Egypt to a point above the fourth cataract of the Nile, the extreme southern limit of Pharaonic conquest. The grandson of Ahmosis, Thutmosis I whose obelisk we shall see at Thebes, carried Egyptian power to the upper Euphrates, but was unable to organize his conquests into Egyptian dependencies. The succession of his daughter, Hatshepsut, interrupted the course of foreign conquest, for this remarkable queen was not given to war and neglected the empire abroad. She devoted herself to the peaceful development of her empire. Her greatest feat was an expedition to the Somali coast on a much larger scale that anything formerly known and, when we have visited Thebes, we will see her expedition trafficking with the natives of distant Punt, as the Egyptians called the Somali coast. Meantime the Asiatic conquests fall away. Finally, after much confusion in the succession to the crown, Thutmosis III the brother of the talented queen, succeeds in maneuvering his sister out of the throne. He immediately began the recovery of the conquests in Asia. In no less than 17 great campaigns he subdued all Palestine and Syria; he planted a tablet of victory alongside that of his father on the banks of the Euphrates, he organized the conquered lands into dependencies of Egypt, built forts, planted garrisons, appointed governors or allowed former princes to rule as vassals of Egypt; and when he died, after a reign of 54 years, he was regularly receiving tribute from the uttermost parts of a vast realm, the first organized empire known in history, extending from the upper waters of the Euphrates to the fourth cataract of the Nile. All that honor which following current tradition we have customarily accorded Ramses II, belongs to Thutmosis III as the greatest military genius of earlier Oriental history.

This position of power and splendor, the influx of untold wealth, the sudden and intimate commingling with the life and culture of Asiatic peoples, reacted powerfully upon Egypt as well in political as in social and industrial life, producing after the reign of Thutmosis III the most profound and far-reaching changes. Before the 18th dynasty social conditions were not radically different from those of the Middle Kingdom, so that there is more of change in this particular, in and immediately following his reign, than during the entire interim from the Middle Kingdom to the Empire. Among many of these changes we notice the vast influx of foreign captives taken especially in the Asiatic wars. They were utilized particularly on the Pharaoh's buildings, in just such a manner as the Hebrews were employed or in medieval days the captives from the ranks of the crusaders, forced by Saladin to build the walls of his citadel at Cairo. It was their labor, though not their skill, which built the mighty temples which we shall find up the river, especially at Thebes. In general, all those changes which affect a people of simple habits when suddenly raised to a position of great power are now observable. Asiatic princesses from Babylonia and the upper Euphrates for three traceable generations and probably longer, are given in marriage to the Pharaoh by their royal fathers. In the industrial and aesthetic arts, in language, in costume, in religion, in pastimes, in war, Egypt is now strongly tinctured by Semitic Asia. Even far off Mycenae, too, is present in pottery and metal work and traffic with the whole northern world is constant and far-reaching.

Under the two immediate successors of Thutmosis III his vast conquests in Asia were maintained with vigilance, followed by some relaxation under Amenophis III, his great-grandson. The thinking men of the time now began unconsciously to feel the widening of the horizon which Egypt had experienced in the last 150 years. Most of their gods had once been local divinities, worshiped only in restricted districts, but they now began to extend the jurisdiction of the great state god Re to the limits of the Egyptian empire. In other words, political conditions were gradually leading them to a practical if not to a philosophical monotheism. Amenophis IV, the son of Amenophis III, provoked the rising power of the old Theban god Amon with whose priesthood he was politically at loggerheads, inaugurated a far-reaching revolution, in the course of which he attempted to introduce the exclusive worship of Re, the sun-god, throughout his realm. For this purpose he established several new cities, one in Egypt, one in Nubia and possibly one in Palestine, each devoted to the sole worship of his sun-god under the name "Aton" which is an old Egyptian word meaning "sun-disk." The new city in Egypt was located at Tell el-Amarna, about 320 miles below Thebes; and, forsaking Thebes, the king made it his royal residence and capital at the same time changing his own name from Amenophis which contained the name of the hated Amon, to Ikhnaton [Akhenaten] which means "Brightness (or possibly Spirit) of the Sun-Disk."

The beliefs of the new faith developed by Amenophis IV are remarkable. The surviving hymns containing all that we know of it express adoration of one god ruling all the world of which the Egyptian knew. They delight in reiterated examples of his creative power, as seen in plants, animals, men or the great world itself, and then of his benevolent sustenance of all that he has created. But they are not ethical; they contain no hint that the recognition of a great benevolent purpose carries with it morality and righteousness in the character of god, or the demand for these in the character of men. Nevertheless, the entire movement was far in advance of the age. After a reign of 17 years Ikhnaton died leaving no son; with him perished the remarkable movement which solely by his own personal power he had sustained against the tremendous inertia of immemorial custom and tradition. The Amonite priests wreaked vengeance upon the body, the tomb, the temple and the city of the hated idealist and reestablished the traditional religion.

The Amarna letters, a series of long-continued correspondence found in the ruins of Ikhnaton's new city of Tell el-Amarna, was a correspondence maintained between the Pharaohs and their vassal kinglets in Syria and Palestine and also a series of letters between the kings of the Tigro-Euphrates valley and the Pharaohs — all affording us a vivid picture of the provincial administration of this period and of the plotting and counterplotting of the petty, semi-independent Palestinian and Syrian rulers, each striving to gain the support of the home government against his fellows. Here we find Machiavellian politics already ripened to a degree of cynical perfection which we should never have anticipated. But the far-reaching disturbances accompanying the revolution of Ikhnaton weakened the foreign administration to such an extent that all the Asiatic states revolted. The revolt was complicated by the advance of the Hittites from eastern Asia Minor into Syria and the invasion of Palestine and Syria by Bedouin hordes in one of their periodic overflows from the eastern deserts. With this latter movement began the Hebrew occupation of Palestine and among the Bedouin, whose invasion of Palestine is revealed in the Amarna letters at this time, we must recognize the Hebrews. The royal house could not withstand the shock and the 18th dynasty fell about 1350 B.C. having enjoyed

230 years of unprecedented power and splendor.

With the rise of the 19th dynasty about 1350 B.C., new conditions confronted the Pharaohs in Asia. The Hittites, foe-men fully equal to the contest with Egypt for the possession of her former Asiatic conquests, had meantime, as we have seen, pressed into Syria from Asia Minor and advancing southward before the close of the 18th dynasty had occupied the country as far south as the Lebanons. Thus Sethos I, whose face we shall yet look upon, after receiving the ready submission of Palestine was able to advance no further than a little north of Carmel, thus gaining the southern coast of Phoenicia. His son, Ramses II, after continuous war for over 17 years, failed to break the power of the stubborn Hittites or to wrench from them the northern conquests of Thutmosis III. He therefore concluded a peace with them on equal terms, having permanently advanced his northern boundaries very little beyond those of his father, Sethos I. One of his famous battles in this war at the city of Kadesh nearly cost him his life and he was fond of having his valiant defense on that occasion depicted in splendid reliefs in his great temples. These we shall later see at Thebes. Egypt's territory in Asia is now essentially within the limits of later Palestine, with the addition of the Phoenician coast cities as far north as Beirut. The enormously long reign of Ramses II (67 years) and the astonishing number of his great buildings made him the ideal Pharaoh in the eyes of later generations and even modern scholars have falsely identified him with Sesostris, the legendary hero of Egypt in Greek tradition, about whom clustered all the great deeds of Egypt's kings of every age. But all the Sesostrises belong in the Middle Kingdom.

Under the successors of Ramses II the Empire, hard beset by Libyan invasion, again sank into weakness and confusion. Among the Semitic captives who in great numbers have been brought into the country since the days of Thutmosis III, the Hebrews must have been toiling on the royal buildings of this age, as narrated in the Old Testament. They dwelt in the land of Goshen, in the eastern Delta, which we shall later visit. In the Cairo Museum we shall see the only monument referring to Israel by name. The scanty evidence would indicate that their escape from Egypt occurred in the decline which followed the death of Ramses II, but there is no monumental reference to their flight. On their escape they were able to join kindred tribes who had been gradually occupying Palestine since the decline of the 18th dynasty.

With the accession of the 20th dynasty, about 1200 B.C., the country is so visibly on the decline that the rise of this or that family into power is but an incident in her decay. The advent of the 20th dynasty under Ramses III was therefore but a deceptive rally. This king, who in every way imitated Ramses II, succeeded in turning back the tide of Libyan invasion already serious at the close of the 19th dynasty. He was notably successful in maintaining his Asiatic frontier at essentially the same limits as those of Ramses II and this against an inpouring horde of invaders from the north who advanced southward by sea and land, devastating Syria as they went. We shall see at Thebes, on the wall of one of his temples, the naval battle which he fought with them. But his is an empty prosperity; affairs at home are in the worst possible condition. The native forces of the Egyptian people are exhausted; their military enthusiasm is forever quenched. From the fall of the 19th dynasty the internal history of Egypt is but the story of the overthrow of the Pharaohs and the usurpation of the throne, first by the priests of Amon and then by foreign mercenaries from the ranks of the Libyans who now largely make up the army. The offices of the priest and the soldier, the strength of the state in the early Empire, are now perverted to the destruction of the ancient nation.

The Decadence
1150-663 B.C.

Shortly after the death of Ramses III, the Asiatic empire finally collapsed and the long Decadence ensued. Ramses XII, the ninth of the feeble Ramessids who one after another followed Ramses III, was unable to transmit the crown to his son or was quietly set aside by Hir-Hor, the high priest of Amon at Thebes. The priests did not long succeed in retaining the royal honors, for the Ramessids who from Ramses II's day had lived in the Delta, set up a dynasty in his splendid Delta city of Tanis. They forced the Amonite priests from the throne and reconciled the priestly party by themselves assuming the high priesthood of Amon and intermarrying with the women of the old priestly house. They form the 21st dynasty. The overthrow of the Ramessids of the 20th dynasty could hardly have occurred much later than 1100 B.C. It brought the seat of power finally to the Delta, already since Ramses II's day the royal residence, and thus the decline of Thebes began. It also lost Palestine to Egypt and permitted the rise of the Israelitish monarchy during the 11th and 10th centuries in a region which for about 500 years had been an Egyptian province. The great building period which began with the 18th dynasty at Thebes was now ended and the vast temples which we shall find there grew up under the Empire, particularly the 18th and 19th dynasties.

From very early times the Egyptians, naturally unwarlike, had received Libyan mercenaries among their troops. From the rise of the 19th dynasty onward, the native forces were more and more inclined to relinquish the sword to these foreigners who increased in numbers with every subsequent reign. The victories of Ramses III were for the most part due to them. About 950 B.C. when the power of the native Pharaohs was at its lowest ebb, these powerful military adventurers thrust aside the feeble 21st dynasty and assumed the kingship, forming the 22nd dynasty. Thus, after some 2,500 years of native rule, the spent and impoverished nation passed under foreign masters and with trifling exceptions she has had nothing else since. From this time on there was "no more a prince out of the land of Egypt."

The Libyan Period
950-663 B.C.

The first ruler of the new family, Sheshonk (Biblical Shishak), early planned for the recovery of the ancient province of Palestine. Hence it was that he received Jeroboam so willingly and seized the opportunity of a division among the Hebrews (with which it is not impossible that he had something to do) to reconquer Palestine and plunder Jerusalem (I Kings xiv, 25-26). The attempted reconquest, apparently little more than a plundering expedition, was not enduring but Sheshonk had a record of it engraved on the wall of the Karnak temple at Thebes where we shall study it. But the power of Sheshonk's successors in Bubastis, the Osorkons, the Sheshonks and the Takelots, rapidly declined while in the Delta and up the valley there was, within 100 years of the first Sheshonk's death, a similar kinglet in almost every important city. Hence it was that Egypt was unable to do anything to check the rapidly rising power of Assyria which was now threatening Palestine. Of these Bubastite or 22nd dynasty kings after Sheshonk I, we know almost nothing, so few monuments have been left us and so complete is the destruction of the Delta cities.

The Nubian Period
775-663 B.C.

While the weakling princes of the Delta were doing all in their power to check Assyria's westward progress, a new complication arose in the Nile valley itself. Probably as early as the 21st dynasty the Nubians had gained their independence and there grew up an independent Cushite kingdom on the upper river with its capital at Napata, just below the fourth cataract. Here then, with an ever deepening tinge of barbarism, we find developing a repetition of the Theban state, with Amon at its head. These Egyptianized Ethiopians soon pushed northward and gained control of Thebes whose priesthood had perhaps founded the new kingdom at Napata. By 732 B.C. they were ready for greater things and the conquest of all Egypt, with the exception of some of the more stubborn Delta cities, was successfully achieved by their first great king, Piankhi. It was, however, but temporary and for 100 years after the invasion the history of Egypt is made up on the one hand of attempts of the local kinglets on the lower river at overthrowing each other, and on the other the invasions of the Ethiopians who found it only too easy to subdue and plunder a nation so disorganized. This situation was further complicated by continual attempts against the advance of the Assyrians. But by 670 B.C., after futile efforts on the part of successive Ethiopian kings to halt Assyria, the dreaded invasion by that power comes and Memphis is plundered. Tanutamon, the last of the Ethiopians to renew the attempt to hold Egypt, again came down the river as far as Memphis in 663 B.C. and thus provoked another invasion of the Assyrians under Ashurbanipal. The latter advanced a forty days' march up the river to Thebes which he sacked and wasted, a ruin from which the great capital of the monarchs of the Empire never wholly recovered. Neither Tanutamon nor his successors ever again ventured into Egypt; the Ethiopian domination in Egypt had thus lasted, with some interruptions, from 732 to 663 B.C. Having transferred the capital from Napata to Meroe the Ethiopian kingdom endured down into the first Christian centuries.

The Restoration
663-525 B.C.

The strife of the local dynasts and petty kings which now broke out anew, might have continued indefinitely had not a new element been suddenly introduced. Psamtik (Greek Psammetichos), a Delta prince of Sais, following the traditions of his family, was enabled to gain the lead by the employment of mercenaries from a new source; these were Greeks and Carians. By this means he rapidly subdued his neighbors, threw off the yoke of Assyria, and by 645 B.C. had gained the whole valley as far as the first cataract in addition to the Delta. Assyria, now nearing her fall, was unable to prevent the consolidation of his power. Thus, after centuries of unparalleled confusion and disunion, Egypt was finally granted peace and stable government and Psamtik ushered in a new day. His family we call the 26th dynasty. Egypt now prospered as never before and in Greek and Phoenician bottoms her products were carried to every mart of the known world. Now began the establishment of her naval power which made her so formidable under the Ptolemies. The Greeks now entered the country in large numbers and were allowed to found in the western Delta their great trading city of Naukratis. This period was in every sense a restoration; perhaps not of the glory of the Empire, but in intention at least, a restoration of the Old Kingdom which had created such enduring witnesses of its power and, seen through the perspective of twenty centuries, seemed to the Saites an ideal age. Although the hopes of Psamtik's dynasty for the recovery of Syria and Palestine, naturally excited by the fall of Assyria, were thwarted by the unexpected rise of Babylonia under Nebuchadrezzar, nevertheless the family ruled in great power and prosperity for 138 years from the accession of its founder. But new forces are at work, the old oriental world is being gradually broken up and transformed, Egyptian and Semitic dominance is at an end and the western world is soon to touch the east with a mighty hand, involving it forever in the destinies of the great nations of Europe. But first came the rise and dominance of Persia.

The Persian Period
525-338 B.C.

In 525 B.C. Cambyses defeated Psamtik III, the last representative of the 26th dynasty, at Pelusium in the eastern Delta. By moderation and justice the Persian kings came to be recognized as the successors of the old Pharaohs of Egypt and, with some interruption, they ruled the country from Cambyses' victory until 338 B.C., almost 200 years. They are called the 27th dynasty and the native princes of the Delta cities who rebelled against them from time to time succeeded in setting up the ephemeral 28th, 29th and 30th dynasties, all of which fall within the period of Persian rule. Of these last dynasties only one king, Nektanebos, succeeded in gaining any great power or the sovereignty of the whole country. This king, under whom a faint revival of the old glory flickered fitfully for a few years, built the beautiful temple of Philae which we shall visit.

The Greek Period
332-30 B.C.

With the overthrow of the Persians by Alexander the Great, Egypt was incorporated into his vast kingdom without resistance in 332 B.C. He founded Alexandria in the same year and it soon became the center of Mediterranean commerce. On the division of his kingdom Egypt fell to Ptolemy, one of Alexander's generals who gradually assumed royal prerogatives and became Ptolemy I, the founder of the Ptolemaic dynasty. The family at times developed great power and ruled the old Asiatic dominions of Egypt as far as the upper Euphrates. Ptolemy I founded in Alexandria the Museum, containing a great library and commanding liberal endowments for the support of scholars and men of literature and science. Such patronage was continued by his successors and Alexandria thus became the greatest seat of learning in antiquity. But his later descendants were often guilty of the grossest misgovernment, cruelty and neglect, under which the country gradually declined. But they were all regarded as the legitimate successors of the old Pharaohs; they respected the old religion and built splendid temples of which we shall find impressive examples when we ascend the Nile in our tour of the country. Finally, as Rome rose, she mingled more and more freely in the affairs of the Ptolemies until, after the romantic career and tragic death of Cleopatra, the last of the Ptolemaic line, Egypt became a Roman province in 30 B.C.

The Roman Period
30 B.C.-640 A.D.

The Roman emperors were now regarded as the Pharaohs of the land which they ruled by means of governors called prefects. Egypt, the once powerful nation, settled down into much the same condition in which she now is. The fertile valley became the granary of Europe and the recognized source of paper, made from papyrus reeds, which it had begun to export as early as 1100 B.C.; but the spirit of the old arts and the mighty architecture had fallen forever asleep. The land was now visited by wealthy Greek and Roman tourists, who ascended the river and admired its marvels, as thousands do at the present day. Christianity spread rapidly in spite of frequent persecution by the Roman emperors until, under Theodosius I (379-395 A.D.), the magnificent temples of the Pharaohs were forever closed. The conflicts among the Christians themselves on questions of doctrine, and the vast number of ascetics in the innumerable monasteries, involved Alexandria in constant broils which, with the persecution of the Jews, her best merchants, made the continuance of her commercial supremacy impossible. With the partition of the Roman Empire in 395 A.D., Egypt became a portion of the Eastern or Byzantine dominion with its capital at Constantinople. Declining steadily in power and initiative, the Egypt of this period has left very few monuments and we shall find little to remind us of it as we pass through the country.

The Moslem Period
640-1517 A.D.

Eight years after the death of Mohammed, which occurred in 632 A.D., Amr ibn el-As, the general of the second caliph Omar, marched against the now entirely Christianized Egypt and made complete conquest of the country. The caliphs governed it with justice and discretion by means of governors, but as the caliphate declined and the caliphs of Bagdad became mere puppets in the hands of their governors and generals, the governors of Egypt made themselves independent rulers of the country and the first dynasty of such independent monarchs was founded by Ibn Tulun, in 868 A.D. We shall later see his mosque which is the oldest building in Cairo. Under the Fatimids who ruled from 969 to 1171 A.D., Cairo was founded (969 A.D.) and rapidly grew to be an important city in the Moslem world. With the overthrow of the Fatimids by the famous Saladin, a Turk, in 1171 A.D., Egypt again ruled Syria to the upper waters of the Euphrates. But Saladin introduced as his trained bodyguard a multitude of white slaves who are called Mamlukes in Arabic. Rewarded with lands by the Sultan and forced to render him a certain quota of troops each year,

these white slaves soon became a body of rich and powerful feudal nobles who made sultans as often as they pleased and no sooner had one of their number succeeded in gaining the coveted crown than he was assassinated or displaced by another, unless he was a man of unusual strength and initiative. They overthrew the Eyyubid dynasty (as that of Saladin is called) in 1240 A.D. and they ruled the country until 1517. Some of them were strong and able men who did much for the country and greatly encouraged art and letters. Under them in the 14th century Cairo became what we shall find it and its most beautiful mosques were the work of these rulers. Christianity, though often tolerated and sometimes treated with great liberality, was also severely persecuted. Islam had long since gained a large majority of the population and the Christians, now called Copts, gradually diminished in numbers under persecution. The old language of the Pharaohs, which had been slowly yielding to Arabic for centuries, now gave way entirely and was spoken only in a few remote villages, as in modern times the ancient Keltic language of Ireland is spoken. It had long ceased to be written, either in hieroglyphic or its cursive forms, hieratic and demotic; for a thousand years the Egyptians had employed Greek letters in the writing of their ancient language as we employ Roman letters in writing English. In the translations of the Bible and in the church ritual this form, written with Greek letters and called Coptic, continued to be used; but by the close of the Mamluke domination the old language of the monuments vanished completely as a spoken tongue and Arabic became the language of Egypt. But Coptic is still used in reading the church service and in the Coptic churches you may still hear the language of the monuments; but the listening congregation does not understand it any more than a Roman Catholic congregation in Italy understands the service of their church in Latin, though that tongue was once the common language of the country.

The Turkish Period
1517 TO THE PRESENT

[Editor's note: the present being 1905 at the time of writing.]

In 1517 the Mamlukes were defeated by the Turks and, although they long continued powerful in Egyptian politics, Egypt became a province of Turkey and a victim of the misrule to which all Turkish provinces are so often subject. The Turkish Sultan's grasp upon the country was often so loose that his authority was merely nominal and, after the ephemeral French occupation under Napoleon (1798-1801) terminated by the British, a young and obscure Roumelian named Mohammed Ali, a colonel in the Albanian division of the Turkish army, succeeded in gaining the upper hand and founding a new dynasty in Egypt which is still on the throne. In 1811 he exterminated the Mamlukes; and but for the interference of Europe after he had gained possession of Syria he might have overthrown the Sultan whose European territory he was preparing to invade. His family has since secured from the Sultan the title of *Khedive,* or viceroy, which is now hereditary in the dynasty. Financial extravagance and hostility to European influence finally forced the English and French to interfere and in 1881, the French having withdrawn, the English bombarded Alexandria and landing, defeated the Egyptian leader Arabi Pacha at Tell el-Kebir. Since then Egypt has been under British influence to such an extent that it amounts to a British protectorate. English rule, however, received a rude setback in the Sudan rebellion. The country on the upper Nile, to a frontier some distance above the two Niles, had been gained for Egypt by Mohammed Ali and his descendants; but in 1883 a religious enthusiast named Mohammed Ahmed who called himself Mahdi ("the Guided"), succeeded in stirring up a widespread rebellion, in opposing which the great Englishman, General Gordon, perished. The whole Sudan was lost to Egypt and the southern frontier was at Wadi Halfa by the second cataract until Sir (now Lord) Herbert Kitchener, after completing the railroad across the desert from Wadi Halfa to Abu Hammed, defeated the Mahdist forces in 1898 and recovered the Sudan. British rule has been an unquestionable blessing for Egypt and the country is now enjoying a prosperity and financial stability which it has never before possessed.

Look back for one moment through this long line of foreign conquerors who have entered Egypt since the glory of the first great empire under the 18th and 19th dynasties faded and disappeared. One after another they have entered and marched across the Delta for 3,000 years; Libyans, Nubians, Assyrians, Persians, Greeks, Romans, Arabs, Turks, French and English. Of all these we shall find some remains as we journey through the country and in no other land can we find a succession of kings and dynasties or a series of monuments embracing such a wide span of centuries as in the Nile valley.

A chronological table will enable you to follow the whole period of Egyptian history with greater clearness.

CHRONOLOGICAL TABLE

Year B.C.	The Predynastic Kingdoms
4241	Introduction of the Calendar.

The Earliest Dynasties (1 and 2); Supremacy of Thinis

3400	Beginning of the dynasties under Menes.

The Old Kingdom (Dynasties 3-6); Supremacy of Memphis

2980	Beginning of the Old Kingdom, with the rise of the 3rd Dynasty.
2445	Fall of the Old Kingdom.

Middle Kingdom (Dynasties 11-13); Supremacy of Thebes

2160	Rise of the Middle Kingdom, with the beginning of the 11th Dynasty.
2000	Accession of the 12th Dynasty, the great dynasty of the Middle Kingdom.
1788	Close of the 12th Dynasty, bringing in the decline of the Middle Kingdom, followed by the Hyksos domination.

The Empire (Dynasties 18-20); Supremacy of Thebes

1580	Rise of the 18th Dynasty, expulsion of the Hyksos and beginning of the Empire.
1350	Close of the 18th Dynasty and loss of Asiatic conquests.
1350	Rise of the 19th Dynasty, followed by recovery of Palestine and war with the Hittites; Sethos I, Ramses II.
1205	Fall of the 19th Dynasty and, after an interval, the accession of the 20th; Ramses III.

The Decadence (Dynasties 20-25)

1150	Final loss of Asiatic conquests; beginning of the Decadence.
1090	Usurpation of the priest-kings at Thebes and succession of the 21st Dynasty in the Delta.
945	Fall of the 21st Dynasty and accession of the Libyans as the 22nd Dynasty.
732	Invasion of the Nubians and Nubian domination, continued with interruptions during the 23rd and 24th Dynasties of Delta princes; the Nubians themselves being the 25th Dynasty.
670	First Assyrian invasion under Esarhaddon.
663	Last Assyrian invasion under Ashurbanipal and overthrow of the Nubians.

The Restoration (26th Dynasty)

663	Accession of the 26th Dynasty and beginning of the Restoration.
525	Fall of the 26th Dynasty and close of the Restoration period.

The Persian Period (27th Dynasty)

525	Accession of Cambyses after the battle of Pelusium.
404-343	Native Dynasties (28, 29 and 30) striving to expel the Persians.
332	Alexander the Great entered and seized Egypt.

The Greek Period, or Dynasty of the Ptolemies

332	Foundation of Alexandria.
323	Death of Alexander the Great and accession of Ptolemy as Satrap.
30	Death of Cleopatra and close of Ptolemaic rule.

The Roman Period

30	The first Roman prefect, Cornelius Gallus, enters Egypt.

A.D.	324	Accession of Constantine; the first Christian emperor.
	379	Accession of Theodosius I, who declared Christianity the religion of the empire and closed the temples of the old religions.
	395	Partition of the Roman empire and accession of the Byzantine emperors at Constantinople.

The Moslem or Mohammedan Period

640	Conquest of Egypt by the Moslems; first Moslem governor.
868	Accession of the Tulunids, the first independent Moslem rulers of Egypt.
969-1171	The Fatimids.
1171-1250	The Eyyubids, or Dynasty of Saladin.
1240-1517	The Mamlukes.
1517-present	Turkish rule.
1798-1801	French occupation.
1805-1848	Mohammed Ali.
1881	Battle of Tell el-Kebir and beginning of British control.
1883	Rebellion of the Mahdi in the Sudan.
1885	Death of Gordon and fall of Khartum.
1898	Defeat of the Mahdists and recovery of the Sudan.

The monuments in the country so constantly illustrate its history that many important events and periods will be discussed as we stand before these monuments themselves. This method will render the great epochs of Egyptian history much clearer, and many of the greatest events are reserved for discussion in the presence of such contemporary monuments.

THE ITINERARY

Together we are about to make the tour of a remarkable river valley, more thickly strewn with monuments of early civilization than in any land in all the world. We are not actually to enter the country in body, but this will make no difference if we can obtain the experiences, the states of consciousness, of being there. Such experiences are obtainable by the right use of the stereoscope and the stereographs. Though we do not actually walk from place to place, still we shall know what it means to stand in one hundred different places in the valley, and if you note carefully where we stand in each case, you will be making the tour of the country with very many, if not all, of the experiences which you would gain by an actual visit. We shall view what we are to see, particularly the monuments, in a number of different aspects.

First, *locality*. We must in every case study the particular part of Egypt we are viewing in relation to its surroundings. With your eyes within the hood of the stereoscope you must consider carefully the various relations of the prospect before you, the direction in which you are looking, what lies beyond a distant horizon, what is to the right, left, or behind you. On the Nile we are especially blessed with important and always present elements of the geography, by means of which we shall be able to locate ourselves. We must always ask, where is the river? On which side of it are we? Where are the eastern walls of the canyon? Where are the western walls? Where is the desert? For these things are practically always with us, as soon as we have passed from the Delta into the valley. Fur-

ther, when a number of standpoints are in localities contiguous or partially identical, we must ask ourselves in every case as we look out over the new prospect, where did we stand in our last position? Even when the distance from the last position is many miles, if you think in what direction it now lies, you will be able to connect the one hundred points of view into a coherent whole, and into a definite progress through the land in a real and connected tour.

Secondly, *history*. Having considered place, we must turn to time, which really means history. In most cases the part of Egypt before us will contain some great monument marking an important historical event or period or a series of these. The main epochs of Egyptian history can be made so familiar to you in a short time that you will be able to place every monument, not merely in its proper locality in the Nile Valley, but be able to see it also in its great historical perspective. The conversation which we shall hold together at each place will be such that, when your memory fails you, the place of the monument will be suggested and recalled.

Third, *art*. Many of the monuments upon which we shall look are valuable, and sometimes phenomenal, *works of art*. Let us always think of their value and meaning as such; let us not imagine that the form of the object before us has always existed as a matter of course, but let us remember that many of the things which we shall see, did not exist until they were conceived by the mind of the Egyptian, and thus a great contribution was made to later human culture, which profited by the genius of the Egyptian.

Fourth, *mechanics*. We shall find in the Nile valley some of the greatest mechanical achievements of man, and indeed the greatest in oriental antiquity. Let us always think of the mighty works which we shall see in this aspect also, realizing that many of the processes employed were first evolved and used by the Egyptians.

If we observe these precautions we shall finally come to see all these things as human documents, the offspring of the mind of ancient man, and frequently opening to us the possibilities of that mind as a literary document could not do however superior the literary documents in most cases may be. Doing this we shall not be making merely a local progress through the country, but we shall also follow the career of its people through the ages and gain a comprehensive conception of Egypt, not merely as a land and a place, but also as a great first chapter in the fascinating story of man.

But the first condition leading up to this mental conquest is to *place ourselves at the point of view*, to obtain a vivid sense of location in the northeastern part of Africa, with eyes in the hood of the stereoscope, forgetting that we are sitting in an armchair in modern America as we look out over prospect after prospect in the Nile valley. If you will but believe it, you will have experiences of looking through a window, from which all that might be seen on the spot will appear in its proper dimensions. In my opinion, there is no other means of obtaining impressions like those of standing on the actual spot anywhere near as perfect as those to be obtained by the right use of the stereoscope. Above all, do not look at a place for a careless few seconds and throw it down in disappointment, but follow with me the points which we are to note together and find them in every case in the scene; and when you have done this, then follow them all through again, noting each detail as you pass it. You will be surprised to find after you have done this, how much each section of the land has come to mean, what an intelligible story it tells and how much more there is in it than you supposed beforehand. If you do this for every one of the outlooks from the 100 points of view, you will have become more familiar with Egypt than most tourists in that country who usually read so rapidly on the spot and are hurried about at such a rate that they bring home only blurred and confused impressions of what they have seen. Furthermore, wherever your memory later fails you, you have only to return to the spot by means of the stereoscope and renew your impression, which the tourist cannot do.

We shall land at Alexandria, and proceed to Cairo where we pass from the Delta into the canyon of the river. From Cairo, after a short study of the town and some of the important monuments in the museum, we shall visit the surrounding points of interest; the pyramids, Memphis, Heliopolis with its solitary obelisk, the quarries from which the stone of the pyramids was taken and the city of Pithom to the northeast, built by the Hebrews. Leaving Cairo and beginning the voyage of the river, we shall visit the Fayum, the great oasis on the west side of the river; and the south end of the line of pyramids. Then, passing these monuments of the Old and Middle Kingdom, we reach the tombs of Benihasan; then the tombs of Assiut, over 200 miles above Cairo, with suggestions of the coming rise of Thebes; then, entering the great Theban period, we visit our first temple at Abydos, and, after a brief visit at Dendera, we reach Thebes itself. Here we shall spend a long time, studying first the east and then the west side of the river. After a visit at El-Kab and Edfu, 50 miles or so above Thebes, we shall reach the first cataract, where we shall visit Assuan, Elephantine, and beautiful Philae. We then enter Nubia and shall stop at Kalabesheh and Kasr Ibrim on our way to Abu Simbel and its great cliff temple. We shall then have followed the Nile River from the mouth to the vicinity of the second cataract. Leaving the Nile at

Wadi Halfa, we shall pass over the desert railway from there to Abu Hammed, cutting off the great bend of the river, on our way to Khartum, but shall make no stop until the last-named place is reached. We shall look at the tomb of the Mahdi, at Omdurman, opposite Khartum, and view the palace of the governor of the Sudan in Khartum itself. Here our voyage will end.

[1] Standing at the southern end of Alexandria we look northward across the city. It was the intention of Alexander the Great when he founded the city in 332 B.C. to make it the link by which commercial and other activities should weld Egypt into the great Greek world empire which he planned.

Under the Greek Dynasty founded by Alexander's general, Ptolemy, son of Lagus, and from him called the Ptolemaic Dynasty, this city rose rapidly till it became not merely the most powerful commercial center, but also the greatest seat of learning in the ancient world of that day. The "Museum," a great institution endowed by the Ptolemies, became the home of the world's great scholars for the furtherance of science and literature. It included the world's first great library containing 900,000 scrolls.

The shaft before us was erected as a landmark for sailors by one of the Roman governors of Egypt and in 392 A.D. one of his successors placed a statue of the Emperor Diocletian upon it which has since disappeared. In the Middle Ages it was mistakenly connected with the tomb of Pompey who was murdered on this coast and it is therefore called "Pompey's Pillar." This column is the only surviving monument of any size from the days of Alexandria's splendor. It is 89 feet high, the shaft alone which is cut in one piece is 69 feet high. In the base, blocks from older buildings have been used, one of which bears the name of Sethos I of the 14th century B.C.

[2] Spread out before us is the city of Moslem song and story, the greatest seat of Saracen art, the home of the Arabian Nights. Under the golden sunshine its soft brown domes and graceful minarets rise against the masses of white-washed dwellings or are confused among the deep shadows and somber walls of sun-dried brick houses.

The masonry upon which we stand is part of the citadel of Cairo, erected by Saladin in 1176 A.D., and its erection marks the beginning of the later Cairo which we have before us. You see the obsolete batteries on the parapets below us on the right. Those two curved salients beyond the guns defend an entrance to the fortress known as the Bab el-Azab.

The most prominent building before us is the superb mosque of Sultan Hasan, the finest example of Saracen architecture in Cairo, and perhaps anywhere. It was built in 1356-1359. The splendid entrance is 85 feet high and the massive walls, 113 feet high, are built of stone taken from the pyramids. Of the four minarets designed by the architect, but three were erected. The one here on the left is the tallest minaret in Cairo, 270 feet high; it is now the National Museum of Egypt.

The peak of the dome of the Mosque of Hasan cuts into the white facade of the luxurious Hotel Savoy, one of several magnificent European hotels now to be found in Cairo.

[1] Pompey's Pillar, the sailors' landmark, and modern Alexandria

[2] Cairo, home of the Arabian Nights, greatest city of Africa

[3] When the great Saladin, the conqueror of the Crusaders, came to Cairo he saw the necessity of a stronghold commanding the place. In 1176 he began masonry fortifications on the height now crowned by that tall mosque and planned a great wall around the city below which was never entirely finished.

The place where we stood overlooking the city is just on the right of the two tall minarets but further back in a line directly away from us. The white buildings behind the parapets of the fort on the extreme left are the barracks of the present garrison. The great mosque which surmounts the citadel with its tall graceful minarets, is the most prominent landmark in Cairo. It was begun by the founder of the reigning dynasty of viceroys in Egypt, Mohammed Ali, after the blowing up of an old palace which occupied the same place in 1824. It was completed in 1857.

The citadel marks the rise of a new vigorous dynasty. The 600 year domination of the Mamlukes was brought to a bloody end when on March 1, 1811 they were, by order of Mohammed Ali, shot down from the surrounding walls.

Nearer us is an animated scene characteristic of modern Cairo, in the Cemetery of the Bab el-Wezir or Gate of the Vizier from which the cemetery is named. Those tents and houses seen in the cemetery are townspeople celebrating what they call the "Lesser Feast" which occurs after the fast of Ramadan.

[4] We are near the eastern limits of the city, facing southwest. That high walled building at the extreme left is the mosque of Rifa'iyeh. Between the dome with the peak awry and the distant sand-hills you notice a horizontal whitish streak — that is the court of the oldest mosque in Cairo, built in 877-879 A.D. by Ibn Tulun, the first independent Sultan of Egypt. In his day Cairo did not exist, but over where you see those sand hills were the busy streets and swarming markets of old Misr. The city before us is mainly a work of the 14th century. It was in the city as you see it from this point that the Arabian Nights, with their charming pictures of the life of the common people, the life of the shops, houses and bazaars, were put into final form, though they contain tales of far earlier date, some of them from 4,000 years ago. Some of the tales which these Moslems of the Cairo bazaars love to listen to are almost as old as those pyramids, of which we get here our first glimpse dimly rising on the western horizon, and which furnished much of the stone for this city.

The two nearest minarets, built within a generation or two of the Turkish conquest of Egypt, are exquisite examples of the classic age of Saracenic architecture.

Five times a day the Mu'ezzins appear in the balcony and summon the faithful to prayers.

[3] Citadel and Mohammed Ali Mosque, beyond Bab el-Wezir cemetery, Cairo

[4] Cairo, looking southwest across the city to the Pyramids

[5] We are in the desert outside the city, looking a little west of north.

These ladies of modern Cairo who are out for an airing, do not seem oppressed by the solemnity of the place. Indeed, as one of them has removed her veil, there is much doubt whether they belong to the class of reputable ladies from the upper ranks of society. What a romantic carriage! A generation ago, such a vehicle was the usual one for the conveyance of the bride at every wedding. With tinkling bells and gaily caparisoned camels it made a brave show as it carried to the waiting bridegroom the vision of loveliness whose face —as is always the case in Moslem marriages — he had never seen.

We look along the northern end of a line of royal tombs which extends along the entire eastern side of the city except where interrupted by the citadel which is now behind us. These beautiful sepulchers were erected from the 13th to the 16th centuries by the Bahri and Circassian sultans, the Mamlukes who followed the age of Saladin. They are the product of the finest age of Saracen art. They were liberally endowed by their builders, each of whom left a large income for the support of a body of sheiks and keepers; but Mohammed Ali confiscated the property of these mosques in the 19th century, and since then they have fallen into sad decay.

[6] We are in the eastern desert, outside the city wall, facing southwest.

Here before us rises the lovely tomb mosque of Kait Bey, built in 1474 by the last of the really great Mamlukes who preceded the Turkish conquest. The powerful and sagacious Kait Bey inaugurated a veritable Augustan age for Cairo, and, brief as it was, the city was adorned with a host of magnificent buildings which today form its chief architectural beauties.

A mosque was originally only a place of assembly in the open air — a square court surrounded by a colonnaded portico. When it became customary to inter the great in a mosque, a dome was placed over the addition containing the tomb. As an architectural element the dome was originally and for a long period the invariable accompaniment of a tomb in Saracen architecture. This dome, the gradual development of the minaret and the addition of a facade taken from the buildings of the Crusaders, gave the tomb mosque a finished architectural unity, which the earlier building did not possess.

See how skillfully the transition is made from the square building below to the circular base of the dome which rests upon it. That exquisite dome is, like the rest of the building, of stone, and the rich carving upon it is the perfection of geometrical design in which the Saracen artist has contributed so much to decorative art.

On the left margin: *Underwood & Underwood, Publishers*
New York, London, Toronto Canada, Ottawa Kansas

On the right margin: *Works and Studies*
Arlington N.J. — Westervelt, Washington D.C.

(5) A "Ship of the desert" passing tombs of bygone Moslem rulers outside east wall of Cairo, Egypt. Copyright 1897 by Underwood & Underwood.

[5] A "Ship of the Desert" passing tombs of bygone Moslem rulers, Cairo

On the left margin: *Underwood & Underwood, Publishers*
New York, London, Toronto Canada, Ottawa Kansas

On the right margin: *Works and Studies*
Arlington N.J. — Westervelt, Washington D.C.

(6) Tomb-Mosque of Sultan Kait Bey from the N.E.—most beautiful of tombs of Cairo, Egypt. Copyright 1904 by Underwood & Underwood.

[6] Tomb Mosque of Sultan Kait Bey, Cairo

[7] We find ourselves in a large hall of worship which, in the original mosque form, was one side of a court roofed over for the protection of worshipers. Attendants sometimes allow visitors to put on some old felt slippers over their shoes, or even wrap them up in some tattered bits of rags which he has at hand for the purpose. But no Moslem would think of entering the holy place on such a compromise. They will remain with bare feet until they step outside the door.

That niche is called by the Moslems the 'mihraby,' and it marks the proper direction for prayer which they term "kibleh," or "facing"; it is very important that a Moslem should always pray toward Mecca. On the farther side of the prayer niche you observe the "mimbar," or pulpit, from which the Friday sermon is delivered every week. The wood carving on some of these pulpits is among the finest decorative designs produced by the artists of the Egyptian sultans. The preacher, who is not specially ordained for his office, but may be any person of theological learning, comes in and seats himself on the steps while the Mu'ezzin enters and proclaims the hour of prayer. Then the preacher rises, and, standing on the second step, delivers a short sermon.

Wherever a man is he must pray five times a day and there is no more impressive sight than to see one of these great Cairo mosques filled with a vast multitude, swaying as they bow down for the prayers as if a great wave of the sea were passing.

[8] There is nothing in Cairo which so strikingly reminds us that we are in a country professing the religion of Mohammed, as the ceremonies connected with this pilgrimage to Mecca, the city where he so long labored.

Every year, at the expense of the Sultan, a fine carpet or huge fabric for festooning the Ka'ba at Mecca is made in this city of Cairo, and we are now viewing the procession which is bearing it from the citadel to the mosque, where the pieces will be sewed together and lined in readiness for the departure of the pilgrims.

We cannot here see the carpet itself, but the "Mahmal" which accompanies it is even more sacred than the carpet. We refer to the curious object which you see at the head of the long procession. It is a pyramid of woven fabric, richly embroidered, surmounting a roughly cubical base of the same material. The whole is stretched on a wooden frame and contains nothing. Brazen ornaments at each corner and a similar adornment crowning a cylinder at the top complete the strange object. Attached to the ornament at the top are two copies of the Koran, the holy scripture of Islam. It is all mounted upon a magnificent camel which is here so hidden by the Mahmal and the crowd that you can scarcely see it at all. In this way the Mahmal proceeds to Mecca with the pilgrims and with them also returns to Cairo. It is the duty of every Moslem to undertake the pilgrimage at least once in his life.

[7] The prayer niche and pulpit in the tomb mosque of Sultan Kait Bey, Cairo

[8] The Holy Carpet Parade with the Mahmal, before the departure of the pilgrims for Mecca. Cairo

[9] The houses of the rich and noble Cairenes give little indication, on the outside, of their interior beauty and richness. As we have come in here from the street, the porter has taken us through a passage with at least one turn, to prevent passers in the street from looking into the court. On two sides of it are ranged the different rooms and apartments of the house; the ground floor, which opens from the carved doorway you see here on the right behind the tree, is reserved for the men, and is called the "salamlik." There the master of the house receives his friends, who, according to Moslem politeness, must not give the slightest intimation that they are aware of the existence of any women in the house. If any of these friends are taken to the second floor they raise their voices and let it be known that they are coming in order to warn the women and give them time to retire or to veil themselves; for the harem, the apartment of the women, is on the second floor. The elaborately carved windows are those of the harem, and there the ladies of the house spend their time listlessly lounging and rarely going out for an airing. They lead the most uninteresting of lives, possess no culture or next to none, and by the men of their own race are given an exceedingly bad character, probably far worse then they actually deserve.

[10] We are standing here in the National Museum of Egypt, a short distance from the great Nile bridge that will later lead us out to the pyramids of Gizeh. Meantime we are to have an audience with this mighty Pharaoh who built one of them. Does he not look every inch a king? Thus he sat in the presence of his assembled court 5,000 years ago and, thanks to the skill of his court sculptors, we are able to view him today almost as if he were in the flesh before us.

That material is diorite and although it is so hard that it turns the edge of a steel tool today, the artist of 5,000 years ago, with his chisel of copper, cut the fine lines of the mouth and the delicate curves of the nose as firmly as if they were wrought in wood.

It was not an ideal conception, the statue before us is the result of an attempt to put the king into stone by a process of exactly imitating his every feature. There he sits, in calm and conscious superiority to the mere human creatures about him, the Pharaoh whose ordinary designation was the "good god," before whom all men kissed the dust and of whom his son-in-law, a great favorite, relates with pride that he was not merely permitted to kiss the ground but by special grace might also kiss the Pharaoh's toe.

[9] The harem windows in the court of a wealthy Cairene's house

[10] Diorite statue of King Khafre, builder of the Second Pyramid at Gizeh, Cairo

[11] Here is the comfortable and self-satisfied Egyptian noble, just as he appeared upon his well-stocked estate, leaning upon his staff as he was wont to do when the sleek herds and snowy flocks were led before him for inspection.

This is a work of the Old Empire and, in spite of the seams and scars of 5,000 years, the whole preserves an air of vivacity which is surprising. But what must it have been when it left the hand of the artist! Its surface was covered with linen deftly glued on; into the texture of the linen was rubbed a paste or stucco, forming a perfectly smooth surface for the reception of colors. This statue — as indeed was all Egyptian sculpture — was colored in the hues of life. The eyes were inlaid with transparent rock-crystal, polished until it shone like glass, in the middle being an inlaid circle of black crystal representing the iris, in the center of which is a silver nail, a perfect counterfeit of the pupil. The modeling of the face is done with unrivaled skills. The right foot and most of the left leg have been restored.

These portrait statues were intended to be more durable bodies, false bodies, which should take the place of real bodies when the latter should have perished. Without such a body the personality would be annihilated.

[12] What would you say if you might look upon the face of King David, of Solomon, or of Josiah? But this king before us, upon whose actual features we look, almost as if he had died but yesterday, lived and reigned centuries before the Hebrew monarchy began. The Hebrews were toiling in Egypt when the utterance of these very lips was the supreme decree of the state. His son, Ramses II, was probably the Pharaoh of the oppression. Those arms, now folded in repose, once bore the sword in triumph through the very land where the Hebrews afterward gained their home. This tall form once towered in the speeding chariot, scattering death and destruction among the Bedouin kindred of the Hebrews as they sought to invade and possess the land of Palestine. It is all depicted on the walls of the great Karnak temple, where we shall see it at Thebes.

The Egyptians believed that such a body as this was absolutely indispensable to the future existence of the person. The process of preservation was easy in a country of so dry a climate. When the climate was aided by artificial means, you see before you what an amazing durability was imparted to the frail body. You can clearly see the masses of aromatic gums and the like that have been used to fill up the interior cavities from which the perishable organs have been removed.

[11] The famous wooden statue called the Shehk el-Beled, Cairo Museum

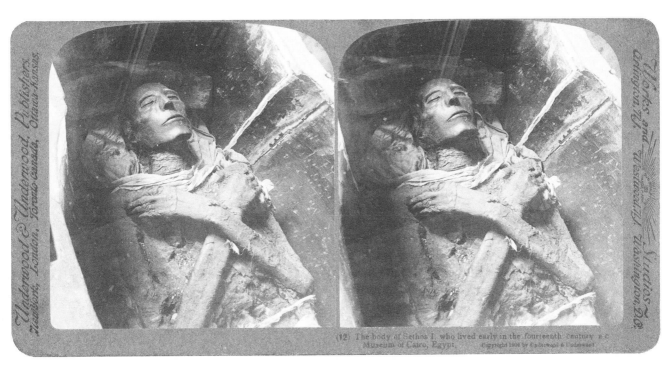

[12] Mummy of Sethos I who lived in the 14th century B.C., Cairo Museum

[13] We are in one of several large rooms in the National Museum of Cairo, surrounded on all sides by treasured remains of the life of the oldest known civilization.

A king was laid away in great state, wearing the splendid regalia of gold, silver and costly stones with which he had been adorned in life. The result of this was that the tombs of the kings, the nobles and the officials, were systematically robbed. Many pyramids and rock-hewn tombs have all been completely cleared out.

These luxurious adornments were found with the body of Queen Ahhotep at Thebes in 1860. She lived late in the 17th century B.C. In the middle is a golden boat resting upon a wooden carriage with wheels of bronze. Within it are a crew of silver, while the figures of the king in the middle, the captain and the steersman are of gold. In the nearest corner is a flexible golden chain 36 inches long, of the finest workmanship. At each end of it is the head of a goose, in gold; the pendant in the middle is a golden scarabaeus inlaid with lapis lazuli. The large breast ornament is entirely of gold; at either end is a hawk's head, and the pendant bands hanging in curves are made up of rosettes, flowers and heads of animals. The rectangular object propped up on a slanting card before the wheels of the boat is a superb breast ornament with a gold frame and inlay of brilliantly colored, costly gems.

[14] This stone tablet in the National Museum at Cairo, is one of the most interesting even here where there is so much of unusual interest. It is hewn out of black granite, 10 feet 3 inches high, 5 feet 4 inches wide and 13 inches thick. On this side it bears a long inscription of King Amenophis III, who lived in the middle of the 14th century B.C. The inscription narrates the king's extensive temple buildings for the god Amon and over the inscription you see the king twice represented as offering to the god Amon. The two figures of the king are near the outer edge and those of the god are back to back in the middle. Curving over their heads is the winged sun-disk.

The king erected this splendid monument in his mortuary temple on the west shore of the Nile, at Thebes. Merneptah razed the temple to the ground and, upon discovering this stela, appropriated it for his own mortuary temple but a few hundred feet away. Placing it with this inscribed face to the wall, he inscribed on its back twenty-eight lines recording his victories: *Israel is desolated; his grain is not. Palestine has become as widows for Egypt.* This is the earliest mention of the Hebrews, their own literature being much later, and indicates that at least part of the people were at this time in Palestine, before they appear as a nation there in the Old Testament.

(13) The magnificent jewelry of the Pharaohs (Queen Ahhotep, 17th Century B.C.); Cairo Museum, Egypt. Copyright 1904 by Underwood & Underwood.

[13] The magnificent jewelry of Queen Ahhotep, 17th century B.C., Cairo Museum

(14) The stela of Amenophis III, raised by Merneptah and bearing the earliest mention of Israel—Cairo, Egypt. Copyright 1904 by Underwood & Underwood.

[14] The stela of Amenophis III, raised by Merneptah and bearing the earliest mention of Israel, Cairo Museum

[**15**] Every day at noon this long bridge over the river is opened to permit the passage of the accumulated fleet. On our right is the city — now quite out of our field of vision. Before us and on our left is the river down which we look northwestward for a long vista.

As soon as the bridge is opened, the craft from upriver pass quickly through by force of the current alone, raising their canvas only after they have cleared the bridge. Then we see the sails of the fleet from below beating back and forth across the current, maneuvering for position as at a yacht race, until, when the right point is reached, they make a dash for the draw. The picturesque triangular sails cross and re-cross like a flock of white-winged gulls at sea; their firm lines are sharply defined against the deep green of the palms of the farther shore.

The cargo of these rude craft is garden produce, grain, pottery, brick, sugar-cane, sometimes livestock, etc. They once carried all the produce of Egypt but, since the construction of the railway and the introduction of the steamboat, their traffic has been much diminished. For thousands of years the Nile has carried the traffic of millions of people in craft like these although they are but pigmies compared with the splendid barges of the Pharaohs. Ramses III tells of a sacred barge which he built for the Karnak temple at Thebes which was no less than 224 feet long, built in the 12th century B.C.

[**16**] We have crossed the river Nile from Cairo, leaving the city behind us, and are facing west. It is nearly five miles from here to those world-famous pyramids on the edge of the vast, yellow-brown sands of the Libyan desert. The nearer one is the Great Pyramid of Khufu (Cheops); the Sphinx stands farther to the left at this side of the other large pyramids. The summit of that tallest pyramid stands more than 450 feet above the drifting sands, where its base covers nearly 13 acres.

The beautiful lebbek trees which line the road on either hand, planted by Ismail Pacha, make the road to the pyramids shaded and delightful in a land where shade is a rarity and the sun beats down with fierce and almost vertical rays. At the foot of the bluff on our extreme left you discern the houses of the modern village of Kafr. Little do the peasants who dwell there dream of the life which once teemed and swarmed in busy streets occupying these very fields. For here lay the residence city of the 4th dynasty, the royal residence of the splendid Pharaohs who built the pyramids before us. Now all that remains of the city is a scanty remnant of the wall. It is not impossible that the first Pharaoh of the dynasty, having selected that desert headland as the site of his pyramid, located his residence city at this place in order that he might always be able personally to inspect the progress of the mighty monument which was to be his eternal resting place.

[**15**]   The great Nile Bridge open for the passage of the daily fleet of cargo boats, Cairo

[**16**]   The road to the Pyramids from Cairo

[17] With Cairo on our right and Memphis behind us, we look northwestward to the Great Pyramid. We stand for the first time on the desert sands. Behind us is a stretch of the ancient wall of the city which was the royal residence of the king who built yonder gigantic tomb. The three small pyramids beside it probably belong to members of his family. In a line with these rises the gloomy head of the Sphinx, gazing into the rising sun and guarding this city of the dead as he has done for perhaps 5,000 years. At the left are the palm-shaded graves of the Moslems, descendants of men who inhabited the vanished city.

How much lies between these humble tombs of yesterday and that hoary pyramid! Already to the ancient Greeks it was one of the marvelous survivors of antiquity, which they placed among the seven wonders of the world; and, although all the others of the seven have passed away and for the most part left no trace, it had stood for 1,500 years when the prophet of the Hebrew Exodus led forth his people. It beheld the fierce soldiery of Assyria scattering ruin and desolation at its feet. It beheld the Persian host pouring in through the isthmus like a flood and repeating that desolation. It beheld the legions of Rome stationed from end to end of this valley and bringing in the new order of the imperial city. It saw the wild hordes of Arabia surging in across the Delta plain as they brought to the children of the Nile the language and religion of Mohammed.

[18] We are looking at the northwest corner of the Great Pyramid. The mass of the vast pile begins to grow and we are ready to credit Herodotus' statement that its erection consumed the labor of some 100,000 men for 20 years. Here we may draw a contrast between Khufu's tomb and those of his contemporaries close to the pyramid at our right. These are but a few of the many masonry structures erected in this cemetery by the nobles and officials of Khufu, who lived at this court and carried on the practical administration of his realm. These masonry tombs (mastabas) are not solid masonry; the exterior is only a revetment covering a loose core of sand and rubble. In the east front there is a door giving access to a chamber where the deceased was supposed to live and to enjoy the offerings of food, drink and clothing which his surviving relatives placed there for him. Besides this chapel chamber there is a second chamber intended to serve as a secret repository for the portrait statue of the deceased. The real body, the mummy, lies far down in a chamber hewn in the heart of the native rock beneath the superstructure. This sepulcher chamber is reached by a shaft passing down through the masonry vertically into the rock beneath. Down this shaft the mummy was lowered on the day of burial and, once safely deposited there, the chamber was walled up and the entire shaft filled to the top with sand, rubble and mortar.

[**17**]   The Great Pyramid of Gizeh, a tomb of 5,000 years ago

[**18**]   King Khufu's tomb, the great Pyramid of Gizeh, and the sepulchers of his nobles

[19] Here the vast mass has full sway over us; it overpowers and overwhelms us. See how the great blocks dwindle as the eye soars upward until they merge and melt into the mountainous bulk of the mass. Here is the very embodiment and potentiality of that ancient state of which the Pharaoh was the soul. Think of the organization of men and means, of force and skilled labor, required to quarry these 2,300,000 blocks, each weighing about 2½ tons, to transport them across the Nile and lift them to the rising courses of this ever-growing monster, till the capstone is 481 feet from the pavement. The base of the sea of stone which forms each face is 755 feet long, and the square which it forms on the ground includes a field of over 13 acres. When you have walked around it you have gone over 3,000 feet.

Perhaps you are saying to yourself that this masonry looks rather rough in exterior finish to be the product of skilled workmen. Quite true; but this was not originally the final exterior finish. When completed, the pyramid was sheathed from summit to base in magnificent casing masonry, so skillfully set that the joints were almost undiscernible. It was still in place when the first Greek visitors beheld the pyramid and wrote of it. It was removed sometime between the 13th and 16th centuries by the Moslem builders of Cairo, who used the blocks for building the mosques and tombs and houses there.

[20] Is it possible that we stand at last upon the summit of the venerable monument of which we have so long dreamed? But look out there on the fertile valley, green and smiling under the brightest of blue skies; then drop your eyes upon this dead stretch of sand at our feet. Nowhere but upon the summit of this great pyramid is therp such a prospect of the most prodigal and unlimited wealth of life to be seen from the very heart of death. Behind us and on either hand are the silence and death of the desert.

We are looking just a little south of eastward, directly across the Nile valley, above the southern apex of the Delta. The Delta, therefore, stretches away northward and northeastward on our left till it meets the Mediterranean. Over on the horizon line are the cliffs which mark the east side of the valley. They rise to the Arabian desert which extends in rolling, desolate hills to the Red Sea beyond. Behind us the Sahara, in a waste of billowy hills, rolls on to the Atlantic 2,000 miles away.

The Nile is that broad white line just under the horizon, coming into view at about the middle of our present prospect and running out of range at the left. It was the river and those cliffs beyond which made possible the great pyramid. The cliffs furnished a limestone of the finest quality, and the river at high water made its transportation possible directly through where the village now stands.

[**19**] Looking up the northeast corner of the Great Pyramid

[**20**] View from the summit of the Great Pyramid looking east over the Valley of the Nile

[21] We stand looking southwestward toward the heart of Africa with Cairo almost behind us and Memphis on our left. Before us looms the second pyramid; this is probably not the best point of view from which to be impressed with its size, and yet, when you remember that the cap of casing masonry which still crowns it extends for 150 feet down its sides, this may serve as a scale by which to measure the rest. Lifted as we are upon the shoulders of the Great Pyramid, we are taking an unfair advantage in thus looking down upon its slightly smaller neighbor. But how splendidly it rises against that background of billowy desert which stretches away southward.

Farther east you observe three low, sand-covered walls, two extending eastward and one at right angles to these. The farther of the two parallel walls is the upper end of a causeway leading from the plain to the desert plateau, up which the building material was transported, and by means of which, after the king's death, access was gained to the temple of the pyramid. The ruins down at the left below our feet are the remains of the temple of the second pyramid. There, in that desolate, sand-covered ruin, once a splendid sanctuary, an endowed priesthood carried on the ritual and worship of the dead Khafre who lay in the pyramid and daily received offerings of food and drink.

[22] Let your eyes run down these precipitous sides nearly 500 feet to the desert below you; you will shrink back, I doubt not, at the suggestion of falling. How insignificant that camel looks far down there on the sand.

Observe those mastabas on the right. Do you see how the central core of sand and rubble is held in place by the retaining wall of surrounding masonry? There was a time when that retaining wall was just a rude circle of unhewn boulders, gathered by primitive man around the sand-heap that marked the resting-place of his departed ancestor, to protect it from the drifting winds. Now, as the mastaba has grown out of the sand-heap, so the pyramid has grown out of the mastaba by placing one mastaba upon another and thus building a terraced pile diminishing as it rose. In the course of time, these terraced sides were filled out in one plane slope and thus at last the pyramid form was attained.

So here we have the pyramid, the most tremendous feat of engineering achieved by ancient man, and there, as its lineal ancestor, the lowly sand-heap that covers the body of the peasant plowman. This is evolution as the archaeologist sees it, and what an evolution it is! Not only in the mechanical arts, which beginning with the sand-heap have finally achieved the pyramid, but also in the organization of a society and government so efficient that it was able to concentrate all its vast resources of wealth, labor and skill upon one supreme achievement, never later to be surpassed.

[**21**] Second Pyramid with its crown of original casing

[**22**] Looking down the southwest corner of the Great Pyramid upon the mastabas of Khufu's lords

[23] Mounted upon the accumulated debris in the middle of the north face of the great pyramid, we are looking up at the opening. Is it possible, you are asking, that the Pharaohs thus advertised the entrances to their tombs and invited the tomb robber in this way to the place where he might gain access to the treasures of the interior? The recollection of the now vanished casing will immediately answer this questions. What we see here is but the wreck of the ancient opening which, piercing the casing just 55 feet 7 inches above the pavement, was so cunningly closed by a single slab of stone let into the surface that it was invisible from below. Add to this the fact that it was not in the middle of this face of the pyramid, but 24 feet east of the middle and we shall understand how baffling it must have been for the tomb robbers. Nevertheless, they somehow gained a knowledge of it and the entrance was known in the time of Christ. Strabo, the geographer, speaks of a movable stone which closed the entrance. This shows that it had already been robbed in antiquity; but it was later closed again and all knowledge of the entrance lost.

Notice that dark hole in the masonry, partly stopped up with stones, on our extreme right. The son of the famous Harun er-Rashid, whom we all know in the Arabian Nights, forced an entrance into the pyramid for the sake of the treasure which it was supposed to contain, and this hole is his forced passage.

[24] We are in the heart of the Great Pyramid, standing at the upper end of a sloping passage. The chamber where the king's sarcophagus was deposited is behind us. In order to go out into the open air we should have to descend this passage and ascend another one, traversing a distance of nearly 250 feet, to regain the entrance.

We are at the top of the grand hall, looking down its slippery slope; without the assistance of the Arabs the ascent is none too easy. 157 feet long and 28 feet high is this wonderful hall, but very narrow in proportion. The gradual narrowing toward the roof is, of course, for safety, as the roof must support the enormous weight of the masonry above. Some of the blocks in the side walls are not accurately dressed on the exposed surface, but if you examine the joints in the first and second courses above the ramps, you will see that the surfaces in contact are set together so skillfully that the seam can only with difficulty be discovered.

Up this superb hall the body of the king was borne on the day of burial; those cuttings in the side walls just above the ramps were probably for the reception of timbers intended to facilitate the ascent. The chamber behind us, in which the body was to rest, is not less remarkable than the grand hall down which we look now.

(23) Entrance to the Great Pyramid, the sepulchre of Khufu (in north face), seen from below, Egypt. Copyright 1904 by Underwood & Underwood.

[23] Entrance to the Great Pyramid

(24) Looking down the main passage leading to Khufu's sepulchre within the Great Pyramid, Egypt. Copyright 1904 by Underwood & Underwood.

[24] Looking down the main passage leading to Khufu's sepulcher within the Great Pyramid

[25] After descending 92 feet along one sloping passage and then ascending nearly 160 feet, all within the vast mass of the pyramid, we come into this chamber to which King Khufu's body was borne 5,000 years ago.

Deep in the heart of the Great Pyramid! And before us is the sarcophagus in which the king was entombed. See how the tomb robbers have broken away the corner in their mad search for treasure. There his body was torn from its resting-place and plundered of its rich regalia and splendid jewelry, then left in dishonor and confusion among fragments of stone and tattered mummy-cloth lying upon the floor. Here, then, we stand in the presence of the most graphic evidences of the futility of the Great Pyramid and of all the hopes that inspired its construction. And yet, what labor and wealth and skill went into it! Look around you here. We have stepped out of the upper end of the great hall, through a small antechamber once blocked by four portcullises of granite through which the tomb robbers were obliged to force their way. This chamber is of granite, 17 by 34 feet, and 19 feet high.

Can you imagine the fateful day when, passing up the great hall with flaming torches, the funeral cortege entered this granite chamber? Bearing the mighty king in his cedar coffin, they laid him in this granite sarcophagus and hermetically fastened on, with molten metal, the granite lid.

[26] We have ascended a ridge of sand bringing into view this granite building, which lies too deeply embedded in the sands to be seen from below. The rough wall which you see on the farther side is but the core of a wall once splendidly cased with granite. Mariette, who discovered the building in 1853, found a well from which he took no less than seven portrait statues of Khafre, the builder of the second pyramid; this building was erected by him and belongs to the same period as the pyramids. It is the massive, monumental gateway forming the entrance to the masonry causeway leading up to the pyramid temple on the east front of the second pyramid. We have retained the term "temple" in the title only to avoid misleading those numerous travelers who only know the building as a temple, which it has so long been supposed to be.

Up through this monumental portal passed the white-robed processions in the departed Pharaoh's honor, to ascend to where the periodic feasts of the temple calendar were celebrated. If we could have stood on the now vanished floor of the roof court which crowned this great gateway and looked down on such celebrations! It is a structure worthy of the builder of such a pyramid and its walls and floors of polished granite and translucent alabaster make it one of the most magnificent monuments of Egypt.

[**25**] Khufu's sarcophagus, broken by robbers, in the Great Pyramid

[26] Ruins of the granite temple near the Sphinx and the Great Pyramid

[27] Its time-scarred, weather-beaten face looks out upon the plain and fronts the rising sun, as it has done these many thousand years, and still we question its mute lips in vain as to its age and origin. Behind it rises the second pyramid, at whose east front we discern the ruins of its temple. In the age when that pyramid was being built, or perhaps earlier, there arose here a promontory of rock, a jutting headland of the cliff which one of those remote kings chose as the site and material for his statue. For you must know that the sphinx, which is a very common form throughout Egypt, is a symbolic portrait of the king. Out of this headland of rock the royal portrait was hewn, and, as it now stands, it is still a part of Mother Earth.

But already in remote antiquity, as far back as the 15th century B.C., the windswept sands of the desert had driven in and covered it to the breast, piling up in vast drifts before it. Right here before us is interesting evidence of the age when this sand inundation had already occurred. Do you see standing between the forepaws and before the breast of the monster that large granite tablet? It contains an inscription which relates how, while he was still a prince only, Thutmosis IV., of the 18th dynasty, came hunting in this region, had a vision of the Sphinx appealing to him, and cleared away the sand.

[28] We stand on the Nile bottoms, 11 miles south of the cemetery of Gizeh. Here, where now the waving palms are supreme, was the great capital city which grew up in the days of the Old Kingdom and became a metropolis of the ancient land. Greek travelers wrote of it; Greek poets sang of it; and in the days of the Roman Empire, it was the goal of wealthy Roman tourists. As far down as the 12th century of our own era, the Arab writers speak of it as filled with an amazing host of marvelous monuments; but after that it began to serve as a quarry for building stone, and, under the attacks of the Cairene architects of the Moslem Sultans, its great walls and monuments gradually melted away. You may go miles over the ground which it once occupied and of all that once made it famous you will find, besides a few mounds, only this colossus and another not far away.

Such statues as this fallen giant here were placed by the kings of the Empire in front of their temples on either side of the entrance. Its presence, therefore, indicates that we are standing on the site of a temple in the city.

This statue is a portrait of Ramses II who reigned some 1,500 years later than the builders of the Gizeh pyramids. The statue as it lies is some 25 feet long, to which we must add the height of the crown which stands on the ground at its head. It is of granite and was brought from the quarries which we shall later see at the first cataract.

[27] The great Sphinx of Gizeh, the largest royal portrait ever hewn

[28] Statue of Ramses II, an embellishment of his vanished temple at Memphis

[29] 15 miles above Cairo, on the west side of the Nile, you find this ancient tomb. The river is now about 4 miles away behind you, flowing to the north. This wind-drifted waste of yellow sand is the eastern edge of the vast Libyan desert; it stretches away to the right and to the left and straight ahead like a heaving ocean. The famous Pyramids and Sphinx of Gizeh rise out of sand-drifts just like these only 10 miles away.

Scientists believe that this strange, terraced structure is even older than the Pyramids of Gizeh — certainly one of the oldest structures of man that now exist in the whole world. This was the tomb of Zoser, an Egyptian monarch of the 3rd dynasty who lived between 4000 and 5000 B.C. His deeds had faded into ancient history long before the time of Ramses II when Moses led the oppressed Hebrew people away from this Nile country and over into Palestine. Even in his time the Egyptians believed in the immortality of the soul and this gigantic tomb was meant to hold securely for all time the mummied body of the king. The material used is clayey limestone and the oblong summit is 106 feet above your head as you stand here.

Crossing a stretch of the desert is, in this neighborhood, perilous as well as tedious, for under the drifting sands are uncounted tombs, large and small, and the shifting of the sands frequently opens old shafts and caverns in unsuspected places.

[30] We are in a hollow of the cliffs at the west side of the valley of the Nile, 7 or 8 miles south of Cairo.

Do you remember those 2,300,000 2½ ton blocks in the great pyramid? This is where most of them were taken out. You will remember that, as we stood on the summit of the pyramid, we looked eastward and I called your attention to the location of the quarries. As we now stand here and look out, you see the glimmer of light from the opening, far behind that huge central pillar which supports the roof.

Now imagine the long lines of swarthy workmen tugging at the ropes as they draw out the massive blocks, the volleying click of innumerable chisels as the blocks are hewn from the mountain, and the hoarse shouts of thousands of slaves mingled with the sharp call of the task-master and overseers when there is any sign of lagging. All this these walls have looked upon as the vast galleries were pierced deeper and deeper into the mountainous cliff. What tales of misery they could tell — of foreign captives by the thousand, lashed to their tasks, driven into these galleries fresh from their Syrian homes where the Pharaoh found them on his last victorious campaign. And now they are forced to furnish the stone to build the temple which shall commemorate the Pharaoh's victory and their own captivity, for upon its walls the story of the conquest will be recorded.

[29] The tomb of Zoser, a monarch of the third dynasty. The first attempt at a pyramid, Sakkarah

[30] Quarry chambers of Masara from which the blocks for the Great Pyramid were excavated

[31] We are about 6 miles northeast of Cairo. This granite shaft is the only considerable monument on this site to tell us that here rose a magnificent temple in the heart of a great city. It was the oldest great religious center of ancient Egypt. Here the priests of the sun-god had a sacred school, from which went forth most of the religious compositions which later became authoritative. The temple was, during the Empire, second only to that of Amon at Thebes in wealth and power. In Greek times it was still famous for the wisdom of its priesthood. Tradition states that Plato studied 13 years here. The city itself was early destroyed, and Strabo, the geographer, found it in ruins in 60 B.C.

Heliopolis is the Greek name for the city. It was called On by the Egyptians, and in this form it is mentioned a number of times in the Old Testament. You will remember especially how the Pharaoh gave to Joseph the daughter of a priest of On as his wife. That priest ministered under the shadow of this very obelisk and it had already been standing several centuries at that time.

Our own obelisk, now in New York, once stood here with its fellow which is now in London (obelisks always stood in pairs at the entrance of a temple).

On all four sides of this obelisk, in a column of hieroglyphics beautifully cut down the middle, are recorded the full titles and names of King Sesostris I.

[32] We are in northeastern Egypt, in a *wadi* or valley which extends eastward between the Nile Delta and the Isthmus of Suez. The district at the west of this valley is the land of Goshen where the Hebrews were given their homes and pasturage. Here, farther eastward, we find these remains of the work of their hands.

Yonder in the middle distance the line of palms marks for us the depression of the *wadi*. The ancient canal which once followed the *wadi* has been succeeeded by a modern canal.

Here for ages the traffic and commerce of Egypt and Asia passed along. Here were the Pharaoh's frontier stations controlling all ingress and egress. According to the Biblical narrative, Ramses II built the city of Pithom, where we now stand. Large portions of such a city are necessarily built of sun-dried brick, and in making and laying such brick the kings of the time employed thousands of foreign captives. It was, therefore, quite in accord with the custom of the Pharaoh to employ the Hebrews. The city is called in the Biblical story a "store-city," and it is interesting to know that the Naville found extensive magazines and storehouses among these ruins. Here before us are the walls of such buildings, and it is possible that the very bricks before us were made by captive Hebrews.

(31) The sole survivor of a great city, the obelisk of Heliopolis, Egypt.
Copyright 1904 by Underwood & Underwood.

[31]   The sole survivor of a great city, the obelisk of Heliopolis

(32) The brick store-chambers of Pithom, the city built by Hebrew bondsmen (looking north)—Egypt.   Copyright 1904 by Underwood & Underwood.

[32]   The brick store-chambers of Pithom, the city built by Hebrew bondsmen

[33] Here you are in the Nile valley of which we have so often spoken. You can see the tall cliffs which wall it in on the other shore; similar cliffs rise behind us.

In mid-river is a dahabiyeh — a long, narrow sailboat of the simple rig so common in the east. Divided approximately into halves, the forward half is devoted to the crew and the cook, while the after half is occupied by the passenger cabin. The cook presides over a tiny kitchen perched like a dry goods box on the bow, just forward of the mast. Ordinarily there are no other quarters for the crew and on the low forward deck they sleep, eat, loaf in the sunshine or tug at the oars as necessity requires.

The passenger cabin in the after half of the boat is surmounted by an awning-covered deck furnished with chairs, settees, hammocks and a writing table. Below, the interior is divided into pantries, storerooms, servants' rooms, bathrooms and a drawing room. Limited as the cabin appears for so extended an arrangement of rooms, it is nevertheless convenient and comfortable.

The workmen just before us are transporting the large jars of which we see a long heap on the bank awaiting shipment. Such jars are made in great quantities in Upper Egypt. Nothing is commoner than to see such a heap as this, only vastly larger, occupying the two decks of a pair of cargo boats lashed together for the purpose.

[34] We are 15 miles west of the Nile, looking southeastward. Cairo is off at our left 50 miles away.

What a picture of desolation! And yet we are standing in the midst of one of the most fertile tracts in the world. These rough sun-dried bricks at our feet form the summit of the pyramid of Hawara which stands in the mouth of the Fayum, and from this elevated point of view we are looking through the valley which connects the depression of the Fayum with the Nile valley. Out yonder on the horizon is the pyramid of Illahun.

The kings who made the 12th dynasty so famous took great interest in the Fayum. Here a depression in the desert of some 30 by 40 miles had been flooded by the waters of the Nile inundation which found access to the basin by the valley down which we are looking. By enormous hydraulic works, continued from reign to reign, the waters were pushed back and the completion of a dike 27 miles long restored to cultivation some 27,000 acres of very productive land. The body of water behind the dike was connected with the Nile by a canal. The modern successor of that canal is visible on our right. It is a natural channel known as the *Bahr Yusuf,* that is, "the river of Joseph" — whose name is thus connected in popular tradition with one of the most important sources of irrigation in modern Egypt.

[33] Dahabiyehs on the river ready for a journey to the upper Nile

[34] Watching a sand whirlwind from the top of Hawara Pyramid

[35] For many thousands of years this device has been used. A pole, with a weight or counterpoise at one end and a bucket hanging from the other, is suspended at a point not far from the weight which then, by its simple gravity, draws up the bucket when filled from the waters below. The apparatus is of the simplest home construction. The necessary poles and stakes are furnished by the scanty trees of the neighborhood; the weight is merely a huge lump of Nile mud plastered on and allowed to dry. The bucket is only a hoop with a pocket of leather lashed to it while the ropes are twisted from palm fiber, as they have been in the Nile valley since the earliest times. With this primitive equipment the native raises the water from 4 to 8 feet, though a strong man will lift it much higher.

When the Nile is low, it is necessary to resort to a series of "shadufs," as they are called, one above another, till the level of the field is reached. In the proper irrigation of one crop, which continues for about 100 days, the native must raise to his field, on the average, nearly 400 tons of water to the acre 4 or 5 times during the 100 days and this necessity keeps him at work incessantly. An acre is usually counted as consuming the entire labor of one man at the shaduf.

[36] We are standing on the banks of the Nile in a typical farming region of the lower river valley.

A small proportion of the Egyptian peasants are able to use another device for raising the Nile waters. This machine, known as a "sakieh," is familiar to us, in a less primitive form, as the bucket- or chain-pump. A wheel which you see out yonder next to the river, as it revolves over the water, carries an endless band of palm rope which hangs in a loop in the waters beneath the wheel. Distributed at intervals along this band are earthen jars which as the wheel revolves and the band moves, are carried down into the water, filled and continually raised to the top. You may see two of them now, just as they are turning over and discharging their contents into a trough concealed behind the masonry. A black horned buffalo revolves a rude horizontal wheel which is geared with the axle of the band wheel and, as the animal walks slowly around, the whole ponderous machine, with much creaking and groaning, is kept in operation and a constant stream of water runs out into the network of trenches which distribute the water throughout the fields.

How necessary such irrigation is you may infer from the parched condition of the soil before us, the clods of which are baked to the hardness of sun-dried brick.

(35) An Egyptian Shaduf, the oldest of well-sweeps, lifting the Nile waters to the thirsty fields. Copyright 1896 by Underwood & Underwood.

[35] An Egyptian shaduf, the oldest of well-sweeps, lifting the Nile waters to the thirsty fields

(36)-2553-An Egyptian Sakieh or ox-driven bucket-pump, raising water for irrigation, Copyright 1904 by Underwood & Underwood.

[36] An Egyptian sakieh or ox-driven bucket pump raising water for irrigation

[37]   The farm where we find this Egyptian peasant threshing his grain is in the fertile Nile valley of lower Egypt.

The rich soil, fertilized every year by the black loam brought down by the inundation from the highlands of Abyssinia, yields two and sometimes three crops a year under irrigation. But the methods employed are the most primitive in the world; they use the same wooden plough which we find depicted upon monuments 5,000 years old and everything else is equally antiquated. Thus, we see them here driving the threshing sledge, a rude wooden affair shod with iron teeth or cutting rollers by which the grain is gradually crushed and loosened from the husks. The straw accumulates in a circle around the path of the sledge as the work goes on. The driver lolls lazily, protected from the blazing sun by a bower of straw and leaves over his head, while his incongruous yoke, a camel and an ox, move slowly around the circle, the dull swish of their feet in the straw and chaff furnishing a monotonous accompaniment to his strange minor song. Behind them shines the rustling cornfield and beyond rise the distant palm groves to mark the pale horizon line. It adds to one's wonder that this people, which became the mother of the mechanical arts and bequeathed them to the world, should have wrought such wonders in stone and metal and yet have been unable to pass beyond the primitive stage in the cultivation of the soil.

[38]   Here is the next step in the process of harvesting in Egypt. The mixture of broken straw, chaff and grain is tossed into the air by the laborer and, as the heavier grain falls again to the threshing floor, the chaff and straw are carried away by the wind. How it brings up the symbols in the Old Testament! "The wicked are like the chaff which the wind driveth away." It is a slow process, as you see here, requiring the tossing of the mixture over and over again; but, as you observe, there gradually gathers on the windward side of the heap (the right side here) a mass of fairly clean grain. Notice how the shadow of the palm falls across the brown grain heap and, as the dust swirls off to leeward and the white garment of the winnower flutters in the breeze, the precious pile that means bread for the peasant and his little ones slowly grows until his comrade, who sits waiting on the ground with the empty basket by his side, may fill it with the winnowed grain and carry it to the neighboring granary built up of Nile mud in the peasant's courtyard. Beyond, under the clustered palms, lie the patient camels so largely employed by these peasants in the labor of the field, and here and there are black buffaloes which in this climate are a great boon to the fellah as they endure the high temperature prevalent here much better than any of the European or Asiatic breeds of cattle.

[37] "Thou shalt not muzzle the ox when he treadeth out the corn." Threshing in modern Egypt

[38]   The winnowing of the grain after threshing

[39] Just north of the chief ancient city of the Fayum, we stand looking nearly eastward over the ruins of Crocodilopolis. Behind us stretches the Fayum, rising at last to the vast waste of the Sahara, spreading out to the far Atlantic. Beyond the trees that mark the skyline before us the Nile is 25 miles away.

Deep down under these ancient crumbling walls lie the scanty remains of a town at least as old as the 12th dynasty kings, who 2,000 years before Christ recovered this district from the waters of the lake. They built a temple here sacred to the crocodile god Sebek, after whom the city was called by the Greeks, Crocodilopolis. When the Greek kings, the Ptolemies, came into power they used the rich fields of the Fayum as gift lands with which to reward their soldiers. Some of the greatest products of Greek thought have turned up among the house ruins, such as the Constitution of Aristotle, poems of Sappho and innumerable fragments of Homer.

We see here modern natives engaged in brickmaking by the same methods that were employed 5,000 years ago. The soft mud is being mixed under the feet of a fellah, while another at a table molds it into bricks. These are taken while still in the molds and carried to the yard by a third native who gently detaches them from the molds and leaves them to dry in long rows.

[40] We stand on ground sacred to the great barons and feudal lords of the 12th dynasty. The slope of a mountain extends backward and upward beyond the cornice of the facade, for we are before a tomb hewn out of the solid rock of the canyon cliffs.

That door before us gives access to the chapel chamber. As it was impossible to hew the secret chamber for the mortuary statue out of the solid rock without leaving one side of it open, the secret chamber thus became an open niche or shrine in the back wall of the chapel. The sepulcher chamber, where the mummy was deposited, is below the chapel, reached by a shaft leading from the floor of the chapel vertically downward.

The tomb is architecturally interesting. Look at that architrave timber resting upon the tops of the pillars. Would you not imagine it were hewn in wood? But look farther at that row of timber ends projecting under the cornice. They are but the imitation in stone of the ends of the wooden timbers which supported the roof in the wooden structure unconsciously used by the architect as his model.

But who was the man who slept in this tomb? Here are his name and pompous titles written all around the door. He was Khnumhotep, who lived in the 20th century B.C. — one of those feudal barons of the 12th dynasty whom the Pharaoh was forced to conciliate.

(39) Brick-making—the task of the Hebrews as seen to-day among the ruins of Crocodilopolis—Egypt. Copyright 1904 by Underwood & Underwood.

[39] Brick making, once the task of the Hebrews, as seen today among the ruins of Crocodilopolis

(40) The tomb of a feudal lord at Benihasan, built about 1900 B.C.—Egypt. Copyright 1904 by Underwood & Underwood.

[40] The tomb of a feudal lord at Benihasan, built about 1900 B.C.

[41] We stand on the west side of the Nile with our backs to the modern town of Assiut and the river, and look southwest. We are now 235 miles above Cairo.

Behind yonder desolate bluffs lies the Sahara, the sands of which have drifted down the face of the rocks and closed many a tomb door. Boldly defined against the distant cliff is the tomb of a modern sheik in the foreground, but it is those distant tombs that chiefly interest us now. There they rise in five tiers, the second and the fourth from the base being almost entirely covered by sand.

The family of nobles who made those cliff sepulchers first emerge upon history in that obscure period when the pyramid builders of the Old Kingdom had passed away and the country was the prey of barons of just such cities as Assiut, each one seeking to gain the throne against his fellows.

One of the largest tombs which you see up there belonged to a powerful lord under the 12th dynasty named Hepzefi. His tomb is of special interest because he recorded upon the walls of the chapel certain contracts which he had made with the priesthoods of the two temples in the town behind us, by virtue of which they were to furnish his tomb and his statue in the temple with certain supplies — bread, meat, wicks for illuminations at feasts and the like — in perpetuity after his death.

[42] Beyond the town is the regular white band that marks the river; the fine white line between the town and the river, at an oblique angle with the latter, is the road from the river harbor to the town — a distance of some ¾ of a mile. Beyond the river you see the valley spreading eastward to the distant eastern cliffs which show in dim gray upon the horizon. Behind them is the rocky waste of the Arabian desert which rises to a range of granite mountains and then drops to the Red Sea. It is but the continuation of the great Sahara which lies behind us. Just at this point the valley spread out before us, which the river has cut through the desert, is only some 10 miles wide. Between us and the town are the fields from which the inundation has just retreated and you observe the black Abyssinian soil which it has deposited. The canal flowing at our feet is one of the important irrigation canals. The road which crosses it from the town is the ancient road which has always led thence to the cemetery, where we are. From the 23rd century B.C., at least, the dead of Assiut have been borne along that road to be interred in or near these cliffs. The ancient town of the nobles lies fathoms deep, buried under the accumulations of thousands of years beneath the busy modern town. In place of their massive temples now rise the slender minarets of the Moslem mosques, brought into the land by barbaric desert tribes.

[**41**] Cliff tombs of the lords of Assiut, the King-makers of 4,000 years ago

[**42**] Assiut, the largest city of Upper Egypt

[43] We are standing on the margin of the desert. Cairo is 335 miles away and Thebes is less than 100 miles distant.

The priests of the prehistoric sanctuary of this place early affirmed that Osiris, the god of the dead and great protector of every soul in the hereafter, was buried here and already, at a remote date, the ground on which you stand was the holiest spot in Egypt as the burial place of Osiris. It was indeed the "holy sepulcher" of Egypt. Every great man desired to be buried here; or if that were impossible, he erected a tablet on the wall of the ancient Osiris temple, the ruins of which are just out of range at our right. On this table he recorded his name and titles and a prayer to Osiris for protection and maintenance in the hereafter. The temple before us was built by Sethos I, the first great king of the 19th dynasty, who ruled in the 14th century B.C. We have seen his face in the flesh in the museum at Cairo.

Behind that row of pillars are seven doors which once formed the entrances to seven aisles leading through the temple to seven shrines. Sethos never lived to see his temple finished; but, on that wall facing us, behind the pillars, is a long inscription of his son, Ramses II. Ramses tells how he completed the structure; one of the things he did was to wall up five of the seven doors. You can clearly see the masonry filling of the three on this side of the center.

[44] This temple within which we are standing was built in the 14th century B.C. and contained shrines to Osiris and the other great gods of Egypt besides one for the deified Sethos himself. This immediate neighborhood had even then been for many centuries one of the most sacred places in the whole land because of a tradition that the god Osiris himself had been buried here.

We are at the southeast side of the second hypostyle hall. Just behind the row of columns at our left are seven shrines of Osiris, the king, and the great gods of Egypt. That of the king is directly opposite your left shoulder. Note the heavy architraves above us; they furnish support for the roofing blocks that cover the hall, but on our left the roof has now fallen in and the fragments have been removed. The row at our left shows a very unusual form, each column being a plain cylinder resting upon a circular base and surmounted at the top by a square block. On our right, the columns are modeled on the bud of the papyrus plant. The bud forms the capital and the stem is the shaft.

The architect's method of erecting these columns is very interesting. When the pavement on which we stand had been laid, the architect drew lines to show where the bases of all the columns were to rest, thus covering the pavement with rows of circles in red paint. Upon the circular base the column was built up in huge drums of limestone.

[43] The temple of Sethos I, Abydos

[44] Columns of the great hypostyle temple of Sethos I, Abydos

[45] This relief shows us the tall figure of the king, Sethos I, as he stands with extended arm, holding in the other hand a censer in which we see the flame of burning incense. His son, the prince who afterwards became Ramses II, stands before him reading from a double roll of papyrus. That little column of hieroglyphs before Ramses, just under his hands, reads: "Recitation of the praises by the king's son, the hereditary prince, the first-born of his body, the beloved Ramses." Whose praises is he reciting? In the ruled column before him you notice a number of ovals. These ovals — frequently called cartouches — contain kings' names wherever you see them on the monuments. Here are three long rows of them, 76 kings in all! Sethos and his son are pronouncing a sacrificial ritual for the benefit of their great predecessors on the throne. This list which they intended for pious purposes alone is now one of the most important documents known for the reconstruction of Egyptian history. It begins with Menes, the first king of the 1st dynasty, at least 3400 years B.C. and ends with Sethos I, in the 14th century B.C. A line of inscription over this list of kings before us states that Sethos is here presenting to his great ancestors on the throne offerings of bread, beer, oxen, fowl, incense, ointment, fine linen, clothing, wine and divine offerings from his temple income.

[46] Standing before the Denderah temple and looking directly southward, we have Abydos now on our right; Cairo is behind us; Thebes, now but 40 miles distant, is before us while on our left is the Arabian desert. Here before us is one of the best preserved temples in Egypt. The part which we see was built under the Roman Emperor Tiberius, in the 1st century A.D., when Egypt was a Roman province. The halls lying in the rear were the work of the later Ptolemies just before Rome acquired Egypt, so this temple marks for us the transition from Greek to Roman domination in the Nile valley. There was here a temple to the great goddess, Hathor, patroness of love and joy, whom the Greeks called Aphrodite, long before Greek or Roman ever saw the spot.

These heaps and mounds are rubbish which was once part of a town. The sun-dried brick walls of the houses have gradually accumulated as dust and mud; generation after generation of such houses rose on the ruins of others which had tumbled down, burned or been destroyed in the sack of war. Gradually such accumulations rose in all the ancient towns until the town no longer stood upon a plain but upon a mound. The temple pavement and the base of the walls are far below the surface of these heaps; the temple should appear much higher — nearly twice as high as it now seems.

[**45**]   Sethos I and his son Ramses II, worshiping their ancestors, in Sethos' temple, Abydos

[**46**]   The beautiful temple of Hathor at Denderah

[47] This is the plain of Thebes. Can you conceive that out there on those vacant levels the mighty city stretched its vast length across the plain? The one-time mistress of the world, the theme of Homer's song, all this she was; and yet you are able to discern her only here and there in clusters of ruins. We see the river as a light gray band, clearest in the middle of our outlook, some 2 miles distant. All this beautiful, verdure-clad valley is the site of ancient Thebes. It was a city of two quarters or, better, it was two cities, a city of the dead on this western plain and a city of the living on the eastern plain.

The city which once stood below us rose to a splendor and magnificence unknown before. Laden with the spoils of Asia and Nubia, the conquerors of the 18th and 19th dynasties returned to this lovely, cliff-encircled plain to adorn it with the mightiest temples that have ever risen by human hands. It was with the invasion of the Assyrians in the 7th century B.C. that its colossal temples fell a prey to fire and sword, in a destruction so appalling that it reached the ears of the Hebrew prophet Nahum who then addressed Nineveh with a warning reminding her of the fate to which she had consigned Thebes (Nahum iii, 8-10). The proud city headed insurrection after insurrection until, in resisting the institution of Roman authority under Augustus, it was taken by the Romans who laid it utterly waste 30-29 B.C.

[48] We are looking southwestward, parallel or nearly so with the Nile which we see on the right flowing toward us. Karnak and its great temple are behind us, beyond which the Nile winds on to Cairo. Before us, over the palms, we see the reach of the river along which we shall pass to the cataracts.

Back yonder where now stand those beautiful colonnades there was once a small sanctuary of the Theban Amon. In the height of the power of the 18th dynasty, Amenhophis III replaced it by a more pretentious temple than any which his ancestors had anywhere planned. He raised yonder colonnaded hall, the columns of which you see massed so thickly in the extreme rear of the temple. Before it he laid out a court. This court he then surrounded by a colonnade on three sides, right, left and front. He planned still greater things. He began another hall this side of the court with the great columns you see at our right, but death overtook him when he had erected those mighty columns which were to form the center aisle or nave of his vast hall — the columns you see divided into two groups by the white muezzin tower of the mosque.

What would have been the thought of the proud conquerors of the 18th dynasty, could they have foreseen the tower of this Moslem sanctuary rising in the midst of the temple court, marking the shrine of a faith which grew up among the desert barbarians whom the Pharaohs despised!

(47 Across the plain of Thebes and past the Memnon statues, from the western cliffs towards Luxor, Egypt. Copyright 1904 by Underwood & Underwood.

[47]   Across the plain of Thebes and past the Memnon statues, from the western cliffs toward Luxor

48) Magnificent desolation—the deserted temple of Luxor, S.W. from top of the first pylon, Egypt. Copyright 1904 by Underwood & Underwood.

[48]   Magnificent desolation—the deserted temple of Luxor

[49] Do you see the top of the pylon tower? It is there at the right of the obelisk. Such a pair of towers, called by the Greeks a pylon, usually formed the entrance of an Egyptian temple, the great portal being in the middle between the two towers. Part of the interior is hollow with a staircase leading to the top. Notice that row of holes made by the later dwellers in this court, long after it had ceased to be used as a sanctuary, that they might insert the ends of the timbers supporting the roof of their house. The other walls of the house were built of brick, sun-dried and therefore friable. As the centuries passed and house after house fell to ruins out there in Ramses' ancient court, it gradually filled with rubbish and crumbled brick until the houses of today, like yonder mosque, stand upon an accumulation 30 feet deep reaching almost to the capitals of the columns. How incongruous the mosque appears, with its not ungraceful little tower, where the muezzin calls five times every day to the worship of Allah in the court of the now forgotten Amon! And all the efforts of the archaeologists have not yet succeeded in dislodging these obstinate Moslems.

On the right are the superb columns of Amenhophis III's unfinished hall, and you can now see the lower courses of the side wall with which his successors closed it in.

[50] The Nile is on our right; we look almost due south. Cairo is far away behind us.

There is not another such group of columns as these in all Egypt. Look at those fine contours as the shaft rises to the beautiful capital. Each column is a cluster of papyrus buds which form the capital while the stems below make up the shaft. The individual stems stand out clearly as well as the buds in the capital with the broad smooth surface below it on which were painted the bands conceived as binding the cluster together. Imagine such a colonnade, painted with all the bright hues of the tropic verdure which they represent, all aglow with throbbing color under a tropic sky and framed in masses of nature's green as the tall palms outside the court bow languidly over the roof of the porticoes, and you will gain some faint hint of the real beauty of which the Egyptian architect was master.

We look into the noble court flanked by that forest of columns in its rear. Their bases are all dark except those of one row which are touched by the afternoon sun. Those stand on the left side of the central aisle leading back through several ante-chambers into the Holy of Holies; down that aisle the august image of the god was borne on those rare occasions when he came forth to celebrate some great feast. The great altar of sacrifice stood in the court before us.

[49] The Moslem mosque in the court of Ramses II, at Luxor Temple, Thebes

[50] The most beautiful colonnade in Egypt, looking across the court of Amenophis III, Luxor Temple, Thebes

[51] We are standing on 25 or 30 feet of debris. If we were standing on the temple pavement that colossus would be some 40 feet high. These natives whom we see carrying water in the old way, not being at all concerned for the temple of their forefathers, are at the same time very tenacious of their rights in these mud-brick houses in which they live. The excavator has, of course, no more right to remove these dwellings than has the surveyor of the elevated road to remove your house in order to make way for his road.

Note those relief sculptures on the left hand tower. All these temples of the New Kingdom are great historical volumes, richly illustrated, in which the conquerors who subdued Nubia and Syria have recorded their achievements. Thus we see here Ramses II charging the enemy in his chariot and, while he draws his mighty bow, he urges his plunging horses directly into the hostile ranks.

This obelisk before us, like the temple pylon, was erected by Ramses II. Its fellow which should stand just before that colossus on the right, was removed to Paris in 1832-3 where it now stands in the Place de la Concorde. As this one has not yet been excavated its exact height is not known. The inscriptions, in three columns, record the fulsome names and titles of Ramses II and a dedication of the monument by him to Amon, god of Thebes.

[52] Up to a few years ago in standing here you would have been looking upon the garden patches of the neighboring villagers where, rising picturesquely among beans and lentils, you might have descried here and there the head of a stone ram. So it had been for centuries. But the government has bought up the necessary ground and you are able to gain some impression of what such a monumental approach to the sanctuaries of Egypt was like.

The soldiers of Assyria in plundering bands have marched down this avenue. Persian hordes have swarmed through it. Alexander's phalanxes have trodden it. The legions of Rome have wrecked it and the image-hating Moslems have shattered its sculptures until, war-worn and weather-beaten, these scarred and battered forms show little of their former semblance and you can hardly find a single ram of which the head is still in place.

Between the forepaws in every case a standing figure of the king is carved; you can see it clearly before the first ram on our right. It is often the figure of Amenhophis III, the king to whom these avenues are in large part due. He constructed them to connect Luxor and Karnak. Beyond that portal the avenue of rams continues to the door of a small temple sacred to Khons, the son of Amon. It was begun by Ramses III early in the 12th century B.C.

(51) The obelisk of Ramses II., and front of the Luxor Temple (view to S.W.), Thebes, Egypt. Copyright 1904 by Underwood & Underwood

[51]   The obelisk of Ramses II and front of Luxor Temple, Thebes

(52) Grand avenue of Rams, one of the southern approaches to the temple of Karnak, Thebes, Egypt. Copyright 1904 by Underwood & Underwood

[52]   Grand Avenue of Rams, one of the southern approaches to the temple of Karnak, Thebes

[53] We stand here at the rear of the Karnak temple, looking north of westward. Out yonder, behind the huge pylon tower, is the Nile and on the extreme left and right you may discern the crest of the cliffs which flank the Theban plain on the other side of the river. Behind us is the Arabian Desert, stretching far off to the Red Sea.

In general, the oldest portions of the temple are nearest us here in the rear and the most recent at the other end. The modest chapel of Amon, built here by the kings of the 12th dynasty, stood out in that vacant space behind yonder native sitting on the fallen block. It was erected about 2000 B.C. and enlarged both in front and rear by the great conquerors of the 18th dynasty, beginning about 1580 B.C. Their additions in the rear are the walls immediately before us while those in front extend to the smaller obelisk, or rather to a fallen pylon just behind that obelisk. On the other side of that obelisk begin the enlargements of the 19th dynasty, being chiefly the vast hypostyle hall of which you see the tall columns in the middle — the chief marvel of Egyptian architecture. This vast sanctuary was completed some 1,800 years after it was begun. Here in these expanding halls we see embodied the career of the Egyptian nation, dynasty after dynasty, till it closes with the Ptolemies.

[54] We stand before the greatest pylon in Egypt. The river is behind us, Luxor and the avenue of rams are on our right and we look slightly obliquely through the main entrance of the temple and down the main axis. Behind and to the left of that isolated column in the court you may see the gate of the second pylon. This is the latest portion of the building. It was possibly erected by the Ptolemies who always favored the old religion of Egypt and not merely respected its usages and sanctuaries but themselves built splendid temples to the gods of the lands.

Look at the towers and see again the rows of holes in which the roofing timbers of houses were supported. The rubbish all around us is the disintegrated mud-brick of their walls. Excavations have been going on here at Thebes for many years, for the purpose of clearing all this away, but there is still much to be done. You see that the methods employed are thoroughly modern, the rubbish being removed as fast as it can be taken out, upon a little tramway leading down to the river behind us. Here, for 10 cents a day, the modern native carries away the remains of the houses of his ancestors to uncover remains of his still older forefathers; the avenue of rams, once completely covered, begins to take shape again and emerge from its long concealment.

(53) The entire length of the gigantic temple of Amon at Karnak, (view N.W.) Thebes, Egypt. Copyright 1904 by Underwood & Underwood.

[53] The entire length of the gigantic temple of Amon at Karnak, Thebes

(54) Excavating the famous Avenue of Rams, S.E. to temple of Karnak, Thebes, Egypt. Copyright 1896 by Underwood & Underwood.

[54] Excavating an avenue leading to the temple of Karnak, Thebes

[55] The tramway now lies piled up in sections beyond the obelisk on the right and the rubbish in the avenue has vanished, though it remains in great masses on either side awaiting a future campaign. The obelisk with the native in a snowy garment striving in vain to puzzle out the writing of his forefathers, was erected by Sethos II toward the close of the 19th dynasty. It was Ramses II who erected this splendid avenue of sphinxes, or really of rams, though they are often called sphinxes. The row on the right is in an unusually good state of preservation and you observe the statues of the king standing between the protecting forepaws of each ram. The ram was the sacred animal of Amon, the great god of Thebes, hence his use as the exclusive figure in the sculpture along these Theban avenues, thus expressing in an oft-repeated symbol the god's protection of the king.

Here the splendid festal processions of Amon passed up from the river to the state temple; but now it sees nothing more impressive than a straggling line of tourists riding up to the gate on such tiny donkeys as this one now in the avenue, while an eloquent descendant of the Pharaohs discourses learnedly upon historical incidents which never occurred.

The gateway of iron which stands open before us is the work of the government for preventing vandalism. The timbers across the door in the second pylon are modern repairs.

[56] What a scene of desolation! Do you wonder that the destruction of this great city stirred the peoples to the ends of the earth and called forth from a Hebrew prophet a stinging warning to Nineveh that a like fate awaited her? The vengeance of Assyria, Persia and Rome and the earthquake of 27 B.C. have wrought the ruin before us and brought low a work which was the pride of the Pharaohs and the greatest architectural achievement of oriental history — perhaps the greatest of all time.

We are standing upon the northern tower of the first pylon and looking down the length of the temple toward the east. Behind us is the Nile. On our right is Luxor and on the left are the cities of the lower river, Abydos, Assiut, Benihasan and Memphis. Under our feet is the latest portion of the building, before us the "great court" of somewhat earlier date leading to the hypostlye hall of the 19th dynasty, behind which you see the obelisk which marks the beginning of the works of the 18th dynasty. Those two shapeless masses of tumbled stone on either side of that door once formed the two towers of the second pylon, built by the Pharaohs of the 19th dynasty. Leading to the door is a kind of vestibule before which stand two colossal statues of Ramses II. The one on the right is, as you see, nearly perfect, but the other has almost disappeared, only one leg and the base still surviving.

(55) Avenue of Sacred Rams, leading from river to W. entrance (after excavation); Karnak, Thebes, Egypt. Copyright 1904 by Underwood & Underwood.

[55] Avenue of Sacred Rams, Karnak, Thebes

(56) The great court of the Karnak temple seen (S.E.) from the top of the first pylon, Thebes, Egypt. Copyright 1904 by Underwood & Underwood.

[56] The great court of the Karnak temple, Thebes

[57] Even in the hazy past when tales of the Trojan War took shape in the Iliad, the Greeks knew about "Hundred-gated Thebes," and quoted it as the supreme embodiment of power and splendor. Now the city which once spread far over this great plain has vanished off the face of the earth, and only parts of its great temples — like this one where we stand — remain to tell of that which used to be.

There are in all 132 of these columns, built of drum-shaped sections and arranged in 16 rows. It is 65 feet up to the top of those spreading capitals and it would take 6 men with outstretched arms to span one of the sculptured shafts. In 1899 eleven columns in this hall fell owing to age and insecurity of the foundations. The debris from the fall has now been removed and the government is spending large sums of money in preplacing the columns as they were before — an undertaking which will cost several hundred thousand dollars before it is completed. The cost will serve to give you a hint of what it meant for an Egyptian king to erect such a hall.

Look at that tiny human form at the other end of the aisle and then set it against the tremendous shafts. What a feeling of littleness as the eye soars aloft amid this forest of giant forms, each bearing its mysterious legend of a forgotten past, of vanished power and splendor, of which there is now no whisper in all the great silence round about us.

[58] There are the two obelisks which we saw from the rear of the temple. The side aisles of the great hall now spread out of each side of the central aisle before us. Especially on the left you can see row after row of architraves with the capitals of the supporting columns beneath them, each capital crowned by the square abacus block on which the architrave rests. The side columns themselves are hidden behind the walls. The side columns are 43 feet high. Those of the middle aisle are 22 feet higher and the resulting difference in the height of the roofs over the middle and side aisles, which we call a clerestory, is utilized for the insertion of a row of windows. You will immediately recognize in this arrangement the basilica hall of Roman architecture and the columned nave and side aisles of the early European cathedrals.

This sacred lake, now the wallowing pool for the buffaloes of the neighboring peasantry, has been the scene of the most gorgeous pageants when the victorious conquerors of Syria returned to celebrate their triumphs in the state temple. In his glittering barge, resplendent with gold and precious stones, the god was borne around this lake followed by a long line of gaily decorated boats carrying the king, the white-robed priests and crowds of the royal favorites, while lines of wretched captives stood waiting to be led into the temple, there to be sacrificed.

[57] The famous colonnade of the great hypostyle hall in the temple of Karnak, Thebes

[58] Looking across the Sacred Lake to the great temple of Karnak, Thebes

[59]   Here we gain a more comprehensive view of the nave of the great hall. The first two columns, one on each side, have been repaired at some period with rough masonry; the four nearly perfect ones on the right convey very effectively the grandeur and somber beauty which an Egyptian architect understood how to express in his great colonnade. Here you see more clearly than before that they are papyrus flower columns. See those vast architraves each supported on the square block, or abacus, resting upon the capital of the column. Those architraves upheld the now vanished roof of which a few fragmentary pieces may be seen lying on them. The roof was 75 feet above the pavement, but all has now been shattered and hurled to the floor below by the successive destructions of Assyrian, Persian and Roman, and what the hand of man could not destroy the earthquake has laid low until the columns rise in nakedness to the sky, flooded with sunshine, whereas the architect intended them to be seen in somber half-light.

This handsome obelisk of Thutmosis I we have seen before. You have been struck by the large and beautiful hieroglyphics of the middle column. Those are the dedication inscription of Thutmosis I early in the 18th dynasty. The side columns of smaller hieroglyphics are additional inscriptions of Ramses IV and Ramses VI which they have inserted here upon a monument which did not belong to them. The decadent Ramessids of the 20th dynasty were unable to erect obelisks for themselves and were obliged to appropriate those of their ancestors.

[60]   We are now looking northward with the sacred lake behind us and a little to the right; on the left, with just the northernmost corner showing, is the great hall above which rises the smaller obelisk of Thutmosis I. Under Thutmosis' daughter Makere — often called Hatshepsut or Hatasoo — this hall suffered strange alteration. She placed her obelisks in it, although she was obliged to unroof it and remove many of the columns in order to do so. She tells with great pride, in an inscription on the base of the standing obelisk yonder, how she did it all in response to an oracle of the god Amon and states that the obelisks were taken from the quarry in the brief space of seven months. As it now stands the great obelisk is 97½ feet high and 8½ feet square at the base, being the largest now in Egypt. Of its fallen companion only this upper part before us survives, but it gives you an opportunity to examine the pyramidal point at the top. This pyramid was covered with electrum, an alloy of gold and silver which, glittering in the sun, might be seen from afar on both sides of the river, as the queen states in her inscription.

The erection of these obelisks having caused the dismantling of the temple hypostyle, it was necessary to erect a new hypostyle. The entrance was erected by the architect Ineni; he says "I superintended the erection of the great portal named *Amon-Is-Great-In-Height*. Its huge door was of Asiatic bronze whereon was the Divine Shadow inlaid with gold."

(59) Middle aisle of the great Hypostyle and the obelisk of Thutmosis I, Karnak, Thebes, Egypt. Copyright 1904 by Underwood & Underwood

[59]   Middle aisle of the great hall and obelisk of Thutmosis I, at the temple of Karnak, Thebes

(60) The tallest obelisk in Egypt, erected by Queen Makere (N.), in Karnak temple at Thebes, Egypt. Copyright 1904 by Underwood & Underwood.

[60]   The tallest obelisk in Egypt, erected by Queen Makere, in the temple of Karnak, Thebes

[61] We are in a chamber just north of the Holy of Holies built by Thutmosis III in the rear of the temple. Here he has had his artists depict upon the wall the plants and animals of Palestine and Syria which he brought back with him from his campaigns there. If they could be properly collected, published and studied by specialists, doubtless many of them could be identified with the life still surviving in those countries at the present day. Here they are, just as they were found among the hills and valleys of Palestine nearly 3,500 years ago. At the other end, now out of our range, is Thutmosis III's inscription about them. He says: "Year 25, under the majesty of the king of Egypt, Thutmosis III, living forever. Plants which his majesty found in the land of Syria. All plants that grow, all flowers that are in the Divine Land, which were found by his majesty, when his majesty proceeded to Syria to subdue the countries according to the command of his father Amon who put them under his feet. His majesty said: 'I swear as Re loves me, as my father Amon favors me, all these things happened in truth. I have not written fiction as that which really happened to my majesty. My majesty hath done this from desire to put them before my father Amon, in this great temple of Amon, as a memorial forever.' "

How the men, women and children — urchins exactly like these lads you see — must have crowded the streets of the old city to see these strange and wonderful products of distant lands which their king had conquered!

[62] We are standing outside of the great hypostyle of Karnak, looking southward against the outside of the north wall. Behind this wall is the vast forest of columns which we have already viewed. In three rows, one above the other, Sethos I, the father of Ramses II, has here depicted the victories which he won in the first year of his reign in the middle of the 14th century B.C. In the lowest row we see the Pharaoh with drawn bow standing erect in his chariot as he charges the fleeing Hittites in Syria. In the middle row Sethos is doing battle with the Libyans who have crossed the northwestern border and invaded the Delta. On the right we see him with the reins of his plumed war-horses tied tightly about his waist as he urges them in wild career full into the ranks of the enemy. He has exhausted his arrows and holds his now useless bow in his left hand while, in his uplifted right, he grasps the heavy bronze sword with which he is beating down the Libyan chief who has dared to face him. The Libyan may be recognized by the two feather plumes which he wears on his head. On the left in the same row is another incident in the battle where Sethos, now dismounted from his chariot, raises on high the javelin with which he is about to transfix the Libyan chief whom he hurls back helpless before him. This is one of the most spirited compositions in Egyptian art and is unsurpassed by anything of this class to be found before the sculpture of the Greeks.

[61] Stone carvings of plants and animals brought to Egypt from Syria by the Pharaohs, temple of Karnak, Thebes

[62] War reliefs of Sethos I on the north wall of Karnak temple, Thebes

[63] These reliefs before us belong to a period long after that of the builders of the great hall. They were put here by King Sheshonk who is called Shishak in the Old Testament, the first king of the 22nd dynasty who began to reign about 945 B.C., that is, at about the time of the reign of Solomon. He desired to recover Egypt's conquests in Palestine which had been lost by his predecessors, and the Old Testament tells how he went up and captured Jerusalem in the days of Solomon's son Rehoboam. (I Kings xiv., 25-26). In Chronicles it is stated that he also "took the fenced cities which pertained to Judah" (II Chron. xii.4). Now you have before you on this wall a list of those very cities. Do you see the tall figure to which the native in the white garment is pointing? That is the god Amon, the great god of this state temple. He wears two tall plumes on his head and carries a sword in his extended right hand while with his left he grasps a number of cords extending to the lines of captives whom you see behind him. Each captive is the symbol of a city; he has no legs, but is merely a head and a pair of pinioned arms attached to an oval containing the name of the city. These long rows of ovals form a list of the cities of Palestine which Shishak captured. The most interesting among them is the name "The Field of Abram," being the earliest known occurrence of the patriarch's name. It is there just where the left shoulder of the native in the white garment cuts into the list.

[64] We are now on the west side of the Nile, looking nearly due north, with Luxor on our right and the western cliffs on our left. They sweep out into view in our front flanking the Ramesseum, the columns of which are in the distance at the right.

Here once stood a noble temple erected by Amenophis III, and the two colossal statues adorned its front.

These great statues which have made the place famous since the Romans first occupied Egypt are of red sandstone. With the pedestals they are now about 65 feet high, but they have lost their crowns which would have made them nearly 70 feet high. Each statue proper is (or was originally) of one block, the base upon which it rests being a separate piece. When Amenophis III set up these giants in the 14th century B.C. they were intended as portraits of himself. The earthquakes of 27 B.C. overthrew the upper portion of the farther colossus and shortly after it was noticed that this statue emitted a cry every morning at sunrise or shortly after. The Greek residents of Egypt immediately averred that the figure must be that of Memnon, the famous son of Eos, the Dawn. He had fallen in the Trojan War and now, said they, he here greets his mother with every returning morning. Visitors came in great numbers to hear the sound and scores of foreigners have left records of the fact in inscriptions on the great statue. Men of the highest rank have thus left memorials of such a visit, including the Emperor Hadrian who traveled in Egypt in 130 A.D.

[63] Records of the campaign of Shishak who captured Jerusalem, temple of Karnak, Thebes

[64] Colossal Memnon statues at Thebes

[65] Before us rise the cliffs that flank the western plain of Thebes. We are standing at the east end of the temple and looking toward its western end. The central aisle leading from front to rear is here on our right and that vast colossus on the extreme right with a native mounted upon it is lying obliquely across the aisle. In the rear you find a colonnaded hall; under that higher section the central aisle continues between a double row of columns. The Pharaohs of the New Kingdom no longer built pyramids but hewed out vast tombs in a valley behind yonder cliff and here, to the east of those cliff tombs, are the royal mortuary temples. Those low mounds which you see just beyond the temple on the right of the four Osiris columns cover great storehouses in which the temple income in wine, oil, honey, grain, textiles, gold and silver was stored; there you may pick up, to this day, the seals from the wine jars bearing the name of Ramses II, just as they were broken from the jars by the temple steward in the days when the Hebrews were sojourning in the land.

When the priest-kings of the 21st dynasty could no longer protect the royal mummies from tomb robbers they dug a secret shaft in the face of the cliffs before us; at its lower end there was a passage extending some distance into the mountain and at its termination a large chamber. In that chamber the mummies of Egypt's greatest kings with their most precious possessions for the after-life were assembled.

[66] We see the white front of the hotel at Luxor on the other side of the Nile. The river flows directly in front of the hotel off to our left or the northeast, but we cannot see it from here because our point of view is not sufficiently elevated. Out of range on the left is Karnak and behind us are the cliffs which we have so often seen forming our western skyline.

The vacant space before us is the second court of the temple with its Osiris columns in front and rear. Those in front now face us and of the four in the rear you can discern only the arm or elbow of one projecting from behind the pillar down here at our left. Through the door, half choked with fallen masonry, appears a peasant just riding past on a donkey as he goes to superintend one of those numerous threshing floors scattered over the plain between us and the buildings of Luxor.

There with his giant head reposing directly in the middle aisle is the colossal statue of Ramses II, the builder of this temple. In the year 1300 B.C. it towered grandly above the pylons and might have been seen far across the plain, but it has long lain as you see it now, a prey to the neighboring peasants who have broken it up for millstones. The native is standing on the forehead. On the right arm, just below the shoulder, you discern the royal cartouche or oval containing the name of the king.

(65) The Ramesseum, mortuary temple of Ramses II.—N. W., toward tombs in the cliffs, Thebes, Egypt. Copyright 1904 by Underwood & Underwood.

[65]   The Ramesseum, mortuary temple of Ramses II, Thebes

(66) From roof of the Ramesseum, past the fallen colossus of Ramses II, S. E. over plain of Thebes, Egypt. Copyright 1904 by Underwood & Underwood.

[66]   View from the roof of the Ramesseum, past the fallen colossus of Ramses II, southeast over the Plain of Thebes

[67] The trees which form that broken line against the faint background of the distant eastern cliffs mark the course of the river whose shores they fringe. The level fields are dotted here and there with threshing floors and in the grove of acacias before us is the favorite well of the neighboring herdsmen. Yonder in the midst of the broad plain are the solitary colossi looking out upon the Nile as they have done for nearly 3,500 years. At a considerable distance behind them you notice a low, dark mass just in line with a heap of white straw from one of the threshing floors. That dark pile is all that remains of a temple. There lies a huge slab with an inscription describing the temple and dedicating it to Amon marking, as it states, the place where the king stood in the performance of the temple ritual. The foundations of the building are undoubtedly still there under the accumulated Nile deposits, at least 6 feet deep, but they have never been excavated.

Here at our feet, as we stand upon the higher roof of the central aisle of the Ramesseum, are the roofing blocks of the side aisles. Our native servant has thrown himself down full length upon them, regardless of the broiling sun and the fact that the roof is heated through and through till it glows like a furnace and the hand shrinks from touching it. The block on which he lies is nearly four times his length — we may call it some 18 or 19 feet in length.

[68] We have climbed the western cliffs and stand in the midst of the innumerable tomb-openings which we saw from the Ramesseum below. Just over the head of the native sitting on the spur of rock you see the mass of buildings making up the group of Medinet Habu. Here at our feet are a few of the tombs with which this cemetery is filled. You observe that the face of the cliff has been smoothed and so cut as to produce a perpendicular wall with a court in front. In the middle of the perpendicular wall is a door leading to the chapel chamber of the tomb which is excavated in the solid rock.

It was these doors which you saw in long rows from the Ramesseum pylon a little while ago. In front of the forecourt Theban gentlemen of wealth were accustomed to lay out a garden in which the deceased was supposed to divert himself, lying about under the trees and enjoying himself as he had been accustomed to do in his garden down in the city. There was not always room for such an addition, but in some cases it must have been of considerable size, for the architect who put up those obelisks of Thutmosis I tells us how many trees he had in his tomb garden and all the various kinds; and they were so numerous that they must have formed a fine grove. Here all around us, then, sleep the great of ancient Thebes; or we should more fittingly say slept, for these tombs have all, with rare exceptions, been robbed in antiquity.

(67) Plain of Thebes and the colossi of Memnon, seen at the S. from roof of the Ramesseum, Egypt. Copyright 1904 by Underwood & Underwood.

[67] The Plain of Thebes and the colossi of Memnon, seen from the Ramesseum

(68) Looking S. over Theban plain and Temples of Medinet Habu from cemetery of Abd-el-Kurna, Egypt. Copyright 1904 by Underwood & Underwood.

[68] Looking south over the Theban plain and temples of Medinet Habu from the cemetery of Abd el-Kurna

[69] The entrance to this tomb is, at present, owing to the debris gathered about it, a mere hole in the ground. This is the tomb chapel which has served as the abode of an Egyptian officer who lived early in the 16th century B.C.

Could you not believe that these colors were laid on yesterday? Yet it is 3,500 years since the artist who painted this chamber stood where you and I stand now and looked over his work for the last time before turning it over to its owner. We are stationed at one side of a nearly square chamber, the ceiling of which is supported by four massive pillars, two of which are just out of range on the right. The whole is hewn out of the western cliffs. This is the room where the deceased lives and receives food and drink from his surviving relatives and descendants — hence the character of these paintings. The owner is everywhere depicted receiving, from a lady standing before him, such offerings as the Egyptian delighted in. In the belief of the Egyptian the deceased was continually, daily and repeatedly, actually receiving the gifts here depicted. If his name were not there the virtue and value of the scene might not be enjoyed by him alone; hence we are able to read his name and titles over every one of these paintings. Over his figure on this first pillar we read: "The hereditary prince, enduring in favor, great in love, favorite of the excellent heart of the king, prince in the Southern City (Thebes), overseer of the garden of Amon, Sen-Nofer, deceased."

[70] We are at the western limit of the great Theban plain on the left bank of the Nile, facing north.

What temple in all the world is so superbly situated as this beautiful sanctuary of the great queen? The snow-white colonnades are flanked by the naked, desolate cliffs with their fine play of light and shadow, bringing out rich masses of brown and yellow against which the clear lines of the temple are sharply defined, producing an effect not to be found in any other temple of Egypt or of any land. No such terraced structure as this is known anywhere else, its peculiar arrangement is unlike any other temple we have visited. You have already seen that Queen Makere was a great builder from her giant obelisk at Karnak. But we have before us a still greater work of hers. The Holy of Holies in this remarkable temple is hewn in the rock of the cliff and you can see its entrance at the foot of the cliff on the upper terrace. It is that dark rectangular doorway over the head of this nearer native. In the axis of the temple, before that door to the Holy of Holies, you see a detached stone doorway out toward the edge of the upper court. Communication between the upper and the middle court is maintained by an ascent or causeway. A similar causeway, which you notice at the extreme right, connects the middle court and a lower court of which you can see only one corner just behind the house of the excavators on the right who freed this temple from the accumulated debris and rubbish of many centuries that had completely covered it.

(69) Painted tomb chamber of Prince Sen-Nofer, hewn in the rock of the western cliffs, Thebes, Egypt. Copyright 1904 by Underwood & Underwood.

[69] Painted tomb chamber of Prince Sen-Nofer, hewn in the rock of the western cliffs, Thebes

(70) Buried for ages—Colonnaded terraces of Queen Makere's temple, Der-el-Bahri (N.), Thebes, Egypt. Copyright 1902 by Underwood & Underwood.

[70] Buried for ages — colonnaded terraces of Queen Makere's temple, Der el-Bahri, Thebes

[71] We are at the left end of the colonnade on the left side of the ascent leading from the middle to the upper court and are looking at the end wall. These reliefs record the main facts of an Egyptian expedition of the 16th century B.C. under Queen Makere, to a district at the south end of the Red Sea, now known as the Somali coast called by the Egyptians "the land of Punt." Solomon traded there later but this was 600 years before his time.

Under this lowest row of figures is a band of wavy lines representing the sea. You notice the fish in the waters. Those fish were so accurately drawn that they have been identified with fish still surviving in the Red Sea. On the right is a file of soldiers preceded by their commander leaning on his staff. At the extreme left you see the prince of the land of Punt standing with uplifted hands in salutation of the Egyptians. Before the Egyptian officer is a low table loaded with necklaces and strings of beads brought, of course, for purposes of traffic. Over the table and the Egyptians are the words: "The arrival of the King's messenger in the Divine Land (Punt) together with the army which is behind him, before the chiefs of Punt. They have been dispatched with every good thing from the court (of Egypt)." Over the prince of Punt we find: "The coming of the chiefs of Punt, doing obeisance with bowed head, to receive the army of the king." The queen regularly refers to herself as the king. In the next higher row over the soldiers you see a large rectangular space with a curved top. That is the Egyptian officer's tent in front of which he stands.

[72] We are looking southeast, our line of sight being at right angles with the river which you descry as a white streak; behind it on the right is Luxor. On both sides of the river the fields stretch away far and wide. Below us, hidden by the rocks at our feet, is the terraced temple of Der el-Bahri at the foot of the cliffs and, if our native attendant here should step incautiously out over these jagged points of rock, he would be dashed to instant death on the pavement of the upper court several hundred feet below us.

That rectangular brick building is a tomb of the 26th dynasty. The temple of the great conqueror Thutmosis III stood out yonder on the plain, beyond and to the right of the large brick tomb where now you see nothing but the level fields of the peasants. There Thutmosis III celebrated one of his magnificent feasts of victory on his return from his first victorious campaign but, like all the other temples in that splendid line, it has utterly vanished. They must have made a spectacle such as the modern world has never looked upon. Having as their pendants on the east shore the mighty mass of the Karnak group and the fine colonnades of Luxor, the whole set in the deep green of temple gardens surrounded by splendid palaces and gorgeous chateaux of the nobles about which were grouped the immense quarters of the vast city with miles of busy streets, markets and bazaars, the whole formed such a prospect from these heights as we have painted in fancy when we read the Arabian Nights.

[71] Queen Makere's expedition to East Africa, 16th century B.C., reliefs at Der el-Bahri, Thebes

[72] From the high cliffs above Der el-Bahri, across the plain to Luxor and the Nile

[73] Here is the rugged crest of the rocks which flank the temple of Der el-Bahri as we saw them from below when we visited the temple. We are now looking down the river. On our right, but out of our field of vision is Karnak; on our left the desert and behind us the upper river. Far down the valley, making a wide sweep westward and in the distance turning again eastward till it is lost on the horizon, is the river which cut out this remarkable valley and made of it a habitable land. Here sailed forth the fleets of the Theban princes against those of Assiut, back in the days when the supremacy of the north or the south depended upon long civil conflict.

These cliffs before us and all that we have thus far seen, are of limestone but, as we proceed up the river and pass Edfu which is 68 miles from the first cataract, we shall find them changing to sandstone, which continues throughout Nubia. With such excellent building material awaiting him on both sides of his narrow valley, it was a foregone conclusion that the Egyptian must become a master of masonry, and thus it is that we find the earliest known stone masonry in this valley. Thus this river with its requirements for irrigation devices of many kinds, and the cliffs with their unrivaled building materials, made Egypt the mother of the mechanical arts, from which the later civilization of the Mediterranean basin largely profited, and bequeathed them to us of this modern world. As the Nile is the real maker of these cliffs, we see what a benefactor to all mankind this ancient river has been.

[74] We are now standing with Karnak and the river behind us; its lower course is now on our right and out yonder, behind that battlemented mountain, are the trackless wastes of the Sahara. The valley at our feet is a depression behind the western cliffs which we have seen from the plain of Thebes behind us.

When the kings found that the pyramids no longer sufficed to protect the body of the royal occupant, they began to follow the example of their nobles and hew out tombs in the rock of the cliffs. The place they chose was this valley and you can see the doors that form the entrances to their tombs. The custom began when the kings of the Empire took up their residence at Thebes. From the time of Thutmosis I, early in the 18th dynasty, after 1550 B.C. to about 1000 B.C., this valley continued to be the royal cemetery of Egypt. The last tomb discovered was found by an American, Mr. Theodore M. Davis. It was that of the family of Amenophis III. In the winter of 1898 M. Loret discovered the tomb of Amenophis II with the mummy lying in its wooden coffin which was enclosed in a large stone sarcophagus. Do you see that open door facing us? That tomb belonged to Ramses VI. Just to the left of that door you notice a pathway leading obliquely up to the face of the opposite cliff. There, in a small bay (which you can see from here if you look at the top of the cliff above the termination of the path) is the tomb of Amenophis II; there his body still lies, garlanded in its ancient funeral wreaths just as they were put there on the day of burial over 3,300 years ago.

(73) Down the Nile (N. E.), across the western cliffs of Thebes, Egypt.
Copyright 1904 by Underwood & Underwood.

[73]   Down the Nile, northeast across the western cliffs of Thebes

(74) Valley of the Kings' tombs where the great conquerors of Egypt were
buried—Thebes.   Copyright 1904 by Underwood & Underwood.

[74]   Valley of the Kings' Tombs where the great conquerors of Egypt were buried

[75] This excavation in the mountain is the sepulchral chamber for the mummy, and the long corridor leading in from the face of the cliff to that chamber. This gallery before us goes down through successive halls 330 feet into the mountain. At the end, in the last chamber, was a vast stone sarcophagus in which the king was interred. The sarcophagus, a magnificent work cut from one block of alabaster, is now in Sir John Soane's museum in London. The body of King Sethos I which was here interred in it, you have already seen in the Cairo Museum. All about us on the doorposts and lintels is the name of Sethos I and the walls are covered with inscriptions describing the career of the dead in the hereafter, and furnishing him with magic formularies which shall deliver him from the hideous and grotesque monsters that beset his path as he leaves this world. Many of the monsters are depicted by the artist on the walls of the galleries and chambers. To enable tourists to see these things without the use of smoky torches which damage the colors, the government has put in electric lights; you can see the wire leading along the ceiling of this gallery.

There were elaborate devices for concealing the entrance and for misleading tomb robbers when they had once discovered the entrance. Nevertheless, these tombs have all been rifled in remote antiquity and already at the end of the 18th dynasty, it was found difficult to protect them.

[76] We face almost due north with the river on our right and the cliffs on our left. Behind us is the western plain of Thebes, for this is the northernmost of the mortuary temples. As Sethos I's father, Ramses I whose tomb door we saw beside that of his son in the valley, had evidently died without having been able to construct such a temple for himself, Sethos I shared his own temple with his father. But Sethos I died before he finished it, and his son, Ramses II, the builder of the Ramesseum, completed the work and appropriated a part of this building for himself.

Thus, it is really a composite chapel for the kings of three generations. The colonnade before us formed the rear of the second court. The two pylons in front of the two courts have utterly perished. Thus we have preserved today only the rear of the temple, from the back of the second court on. The colonnade is built of clustered papyrus bud columns. In the wall behind these columns are three doors; you can see the one in the middle and the one at this end, but the door at the other end is concealed by the columns. This first door leads to the chapel of the grandfather Ramses I; the middle door leads to the main sanctuary, that of the father, Sethos I; the farthest door, which we cannot see, leads to the hall of the grandson, Ramses II. The main sanctuary is also sacred to Amon, as all these mortuary chapels were dedicated both to the dead king and to Amon, the state god.

This temple marks for us the beginning of the 19th dynasty, in the middle of the 14th century B.C.

(75) Descending gallery in tomb of Sethos I., Valley of the Kings' tombs, Thebes, Egypt. Copyright 1904 by Underwood & Underwood.

[75] Descending gallery in the tomb of Sethos I, Valley of the Kings' Tombs, Thebes

(76) Looking north to the mortuary temple of Sethos I., at Thebes, Egypt. Copyright 1904 by Underwood & Underwood.

[76] Looking north to the mortuary temple of Sethos I at Thebes

[77] On our right is the southern end of the western plain, beyond which are Luxor and the Nile. This is the best preserved temple which we have yet seen.

The pylon shows the panels for the reception of the great flagstaves, but the colossal statues of the king which usually rise before the pylon are missing. The pylon itself bears two symmetrical representations, one on the front of each tower outside of the panels. There in relief we see the king slaying his captives before Amon. The god presents to King Ramses III a list of cities and countries which covers the whole front of the pylon below them and embraces almost all such names known to the Egyptions, which the accommodating scribe who put together the list for the king copied from the similar lists he found at Karnak, without stopping to inquire whether the king had ever really campaigned in those countries. The temple is a chronological record of the reign of this king, which contains some of the most severe wars through which Egypt ever passed. Those in the rear of the temple which we cannot see from here contain records of his great war with the Libyans. In the middle we find the accounts of his dangerous war with the sea peoples of the north. As his temple grew, the king was always passing through or had just concluded some great war which found a place on the walls.

The reliefs on this side of the temple, on the outside of the wall, are devoted to the peaceful pursuits and religious duties of the king.

[78] This is one of the most spirited scenes that an Egyptian sculptor ever wrought. The king, with reins slackened and hanging in a distinct curve from his waist, urges on his plumed horses as they dash after the great bull, plunging through the reeds in the vain endeavor to escape to the river. Poising his long lance ready for the fatal thrust, the eager Pharaoh leans far over the front of his chariot; as he strains to reach the fleeing prey he has placed one foot out upon the chariot pole. Beneath the horses we see a victim brought down upon his back with the noose of a lasso around his hind legs and two broken lances in his body; further away in the thicket is another with head thrown back in the convulsions of death and feet pawing the air. The river itself which occupies the lower right hand corner is filled with fish and toward its curving shore marches a line of the king's archers, some of them assisting him with an occasional shaft.

In such pastimes as these the warlike Pharaohs of the Empire were wont to spend their time, when war, the cares of state or the waning attractions of the harem permitted.

Now imagine the river colored blue, the waving reeds green, the bulls a mottled brown with white bellies, the horses white, the Pharaoh brown with white linen kilt, and the chariot in all the gayest of hues, and you will gain a hint of the original effect of this sculpture. It was no common master who put this scene upon the wall.

(77) The first pylon of Ramses III.'s great mortuary temple at Medinet Habu (view N.), Thebes, Egypt.

[77] The first pylon of Ramses III's great mortuary temple at Medinet Habu, Thebes

(78) The hunting of the wild bull, depicted on temple wall of Ramses III, Medinet Habu, Thebes, Egypt.

[78] The hunting of the wild bull, depicted on the temple wall of Ramses III, Medinet Habu, Thebes

[79] This is the massive side wall of the temple enclosing the second court. At the top of the wall, in hieroglyphics over two feet high, is a long inscription reciting the power and might of the Pharaoh and below are exploits which justify this laudation. You see the king's grooms over the door holding the royal horses. The chariot to which they are harnessed is empty and idle but the usual occupant is far from idle. Do you observe him standing just behind the chariot, a heroic figure towering above all his attendants, as with drawn bow he discharges a hail of arrows among the foe? The latter you can hardly discern, but they are of the greatest interest, for that apparently bare space before the king and his companions is occupied by a mass of struggling ships forming the earliest known representation of a naval battle. From here you can make out the forms of the ships looking like new moons; one on a level with the king's feet at the left is especially clear. The enemy who is thus attacking the king's fleet is called "people of the sea" in the inscriptions. One tribe, defeated at this time or later, settled on the coast of Palestine and became the Philistines of Hebrew times. They are Cretans.

At the right of the door we see Ramses III in his chariot, engaged in a lion hunt. Each of the numerous reliefs is accompanied by inscriptions telling who the enemy is, sometimes when the battle took place and often exactly how many of the enemy was killed and taken prisoner.

[80] We have taken up our position on the eastern cliffs and look across the eastern plain, the river and the fields on the other side, to the distant western cliffs. Thebes is now 44 miles off to our right; Cairo is 398 miles away.

That somber gray wall, beginning on the left and extending as far as the eye can follow on the right, is the fortified wall of the city of El Kab known to the ancient Egyptians as Nekhab. It is the only city wall, practically intact, which has survived from such a remote age in any country; for it was erected at least in the days of Abraham, not less than 2,000 years before Christ, and possibly much earlier. You will not wonder that it has survived when you know that it is nearly 40 feet thick. It encloses a space over 1,800 feet long and almost as wide. The interest and importance attached to the city are due to the fact that it was the capital of that enormously ancient kingdom of Upper Egypt which existed here before it was united with the Delta kingdom and the two merged into one nation of Egypt. In historic times the city was the seat of a family of powerful barons who had much to do with the rise of Thebes. Their tombs fill the cliffs here all about us and the walls of their chambers bear many a heroic story of battle and victory in the Pharaoh's cause.

(79) Scenes of battle and the chase on wall of temple of Ramses III., Medinet Habu, Thebes, Egypt. Copyright 1904 by Underwood & Underwood.

[79] Scenes of battle and the chase, carved on the temple wall of Ramses III, Medinet Habu, Thebes

(80) Walled city of El Kab, ancient capital of Upper Egypt, S. W., from the door of a cliff-tomb, Egypt. Copyright 1904 by Underwood & Underwood.

[80] Walled city of El Kab, ancient capital of Upper Egypt, from the door of a cliff tomb

[**81**]   There is no ancient temple which can compare with this in preservation. There was, of course, a much older temple on this spot, but this present building was begun by Ptolemy III in 237 B.C. and completed as it now is in 57 B.C. It is constructed of sandstone. We are looking across the court eastward to the palms that fringe the river and the eastern cliffs rising behind them. Behind the temple are a few whitewashed houses of modern Edfu with a palm or two swaying lazily in the courts, while at the right rises the minaret of the modern village mosque. This is the first Ptolemaic temple we have visited, although the temple of Denderah was begun under the Ptolemies. The top of the towers is gained by a staircase within. Two doors in the back of the pylon, leading from the inner staircases to the top of the wall of the court, you can clearly see from here. Higher up in the back of the pylon and here at the end are the windows by which the stairway of 242 steps is lighted.

The monotonous reliefs on the pylon, repeated over and over again, represent King Neos Dionysos (80-52 B.C.), offering before Horus and Hathor, and their son the young Horus, the divinities of this temple. For the Ptolemies did not record their warlike exploits on the walls of their temples as did the early Pharaohs.

[**82**]   What a superb landscape! The broad plain, broken up into fertile fields and sprinkled with graceful palms and fleecy acacias, merges into the ample bosom of the river with its picturesque sail, behind which the yellow cliffs mingle with the pale skyline beyond. The soft lines of the land-scape contrast strongly with the sharp rectangular contours of the houses of the town, some of them looking very modern indeed with glazed windows and hinged shutters. With the exception of such modern innovations as these, it is not probable that the appearance of the town was very much different when this temple was built.

We stand on the western pylon and look northward. On our right is the river which we see lower down on its long journey to Cairo and the sea. On our left is the western desert.

At our feet is the first court; you notice on the right the colonnade of the portico which surrounds the court. Behind is the vestibule. Several blocks in the roof over the central aisle have fallen in and another which is cracked has been supported by an iron rod. Back of this vestibule is the hypostyle. You can dimly see its door if you look through the central aisle. The roof drops from the vestibule to the hypostyle, back of which are two smaller vestibules or ante-chambers which give access to the Holy of Holies. You can locate this last very easily, as two of the blocks in its roof have fallen in — making a hole so symmetrically placed that it looks as if it were an intentional skylight.

(81) The Pylon and Court of the temple of Horus at Edfu (looking E. to the Nile)—Egypt. Copyright 1904 by Underwood & Underwood.

[81]   The Pylon and Court of the temple of Horus at Edfu

(82) The wonderfully preserved temple of Edfu, seen (N.) from top of first pylon—Egypt. Copyright 1904 by Underwood & Underwood.

[82]   The wonderfully preserved temple of Edfu

[83] This broad band of sunshine falls through a square hole in the roof. We are now standing where only the king and high priest were allowed to enter, in the Holy of Holies of the great Horus Temple at Edfu. What would the priestly custodians, who kept this place inviolate, have said could they have known that our profane feet would one day desecrate this place? Here we may enter with none to stay us, where the sacred processions stopped as the high priest went in to perform the daily ritual before the god in the holy place, while on the great feast days a multitude of this man's ancestors thronged the court outside. They were simple villagers like him but they never saw the interior of this holy chamber.

When was the last service performed here? The edict of the Roman Emperor Theodosius, in 378 A.D. forbade all further worship of the old gods, enjoined the closing of all their temples and at least nominal adherence to Christianity; but the edict could not at that time be enforced here in Upper Egypt. The service of Horus in this temple may have gone on for a hundred years more, languishing year by year as the temple revenues decreased.

The walls are covered with the closely written hieroglyphics of the Ptolemaic age; the reliefs show the king before one of the gods of the temple making offering and sacrifice. On the left is the very shrine in which the sacred image of the god was kept, now open, bare and empty. It is cut out of one block of granite from the first cataract and you see around the edge of the doorway the jamb against which the solid bronze doors once closed.

[84] The first cataract of the Nile is over yonder on the right, above the islands where the native boy is pointing. We look southward across the river, the northern end of the Island of Elephantine, the little "Island of the Sirdar" in the foreground and the modern town of Assuan on the other or eastern shore. On the other shore you see the wild and tumbled surface of the eastern desert stretching far away to the desolate horizon; behind us is the Sahara, even more melancholy and forbidding.

The town of Assuan has long marked the southern limit of Egypt proper. Its name is very ancient; it is mentioned in the Old Testament (Ezek. xxix.10; xxx. 6) and was known to the Greeks as Syene, but occurs long before Greek or Old Testament times in Egyptian inscriptions.

The important town of early Egyptian times was located on the large island out there, at its further end and, like the island, was called "Elephant town." Far back in the days of the pyramid builders it was the southern frontier town of the kingdom through which passed the trade of Nubia in ebony, ivory (explaining its name), gold and ostrich feathers. The nobles who lived here were employed by the Pharaoh in trading expeditions in the remote south — perhaps as far as Sudan. They were the frontiersmen of that ancient day. Family letters of these remote borders have been found in the ruins of their houses on the island. They are now preserved, written on papyrus, in the Berlin Museum.

(83) The Holy of Holies and the granite shrine for the divine image—temple of Edfu, Egypt. Copyright 1904 by Underwood & Underwood.

[83]   The Holy of Holies and granite shrine for the divine image, temple of Edfu

(84) Assuan and the Island of Elephantine (S.), from the western cliffs of the cemetery—Egypt.   Copyright 1904 by Underwood & Underwood.

[84]   Assuan and the island of Elephantine from the western cliffs of the cemetery

[85] We have seen the island where the adventurous noblemen lived their strenuous lives; we have now before us the tomb in which one of the most noted of them was buried. Above is the crest of the cliff where we have just been standing; the river with Assuan and the islands is behind us.

This door gives access to a chapel chamber such as we have so often seen before and it ushers us again into the age of the pyramid builders of the Old Kingdom. The man who built it, a nobleman named Harkhuf, lived under the kings of the 6th dynasty. The place where we now are was then a region liable to frequent invasion from the turbulent Nubian tribes, and it was the business of such noblemen to maintain the frontier and superintend the traffic of the Pharaoh with the regions of the south. Here on the front wall of his tomb Harkhuf has left a remarkable record of his life, telling us the adventures incident to his active career, as he served the Pharaohs of 4,500 years ago. He narrates his great trading expeditions which he personally conducted, the earliest African explorer of whom we know anything. He discovered one of the pygmies which have so astonished modern explorers of Africa, and brought the tiny midget back to Egypt with him. This so delighted the king that he wrote Harkhuf a special letter expressing his gratification. Harkhuf was so proud of this letter that he had it engraved on the front of his tomb, and to this fact we owe the preservation of the oldest royal letter in the world.

[86] On the southeast side of Elephantine Island is this interesting device for measuring the inundations. After ages of use the ancient instrument was cleaned out and restored to service by Ismail Pacha in 1870. It is very important at each stage of the inundation to know whether the rise is equaling that of good years, or whether it is likely to fall short and cause famine and distress. It is difficult to determine how old this instrument on Elephantine is, but it is at least over 2,000 years old, for Strabo visited here and described it accurately. He says: "The Nilometer is a well, built of regular hewn stones, on the bank of the Nile in which is recorded the rise of the stream — not only the maximum, but also the minimum and average rise, for the water in the well rises and falls with the stream. On the sides of the well are marks measuring the height sufficient for the irrigation and the other water levels. These are observed and published for general information. This is of importance to the peasants for the management of the water, the embankments, the canals, etc."

Down at the bottom where the boy stands, the masonry is open to the river, so that as Strabo says, the water in here rises with the rise of the stream. You can see the graduated marks of which he speaks on the side wall, marking the depth at any given level of the surface. The one at the top with oblique lines of white spots is modern Arabic.

[85] Tomb of Harkhuf, a frontier baron in the days of the pyramid builders, Assuan

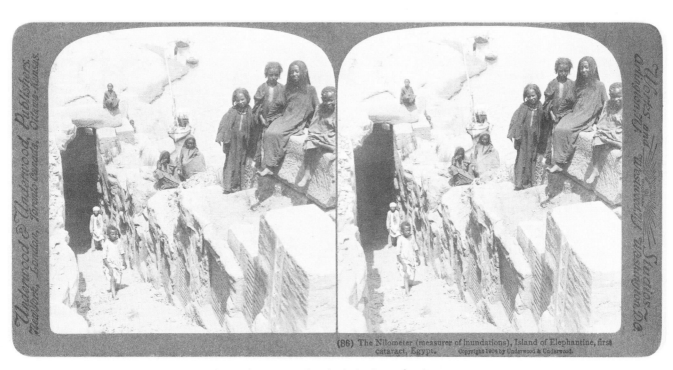

[86] The Nilometer (measurer of inundations), Island of Elephantine, first cataract

[87]   These granite quarries where the Egyptians found stone suitable for their buildings lie on the east bank of the Nile, a few miles south of Assuan.

Recall the huge obelisks which we have seen at Heliopolis, Karnak and Luxor, for we are now in the quarry from which those vast monoliths came. This prostrate giant has never known what it is to stand; he is still a part of Mother Earth from which he has never been separated. If he could be placed erect, he would show a stature of 92 feet which would place him among the tallest obelisks known. All the obelisks that we have seen once lay here as you see this one.

The method of separating it from the rock of the quarry is interesting. A row of holes was drilled along the lower edge where the obelisk joins the quarry rock; into these holes wooden wedges were firmly driven and water was then poured into the wedges. The swelling of the wood then gently but irresistibly forced off the obelisk and cracked it from the native rock beneath. It was then dragged upon a huge sledge to the neighboring river and loaded upon a barge, preparatory to floating it down the river.

The reliefs of Queen Makere at Der el-Bahri show two of her obelisks being towed upon a huge barge; the galleys by which the barge is towed are 30 in number and have on the average 32 oarsmen in each, making some 960 oarsmen in all.

[88]   The inscription before us is on an island in the very middle of the cataract. The rocks on these islands are covered with inscriptions. They form the most ancient and most interesting visitors' book in the world. Century after century and dynasty after dynasty from 2700 B.C. onward through Roman times, kings and nobles, scribes and officers have left their record here.

The inscription before us purports to be an official communication from King Zoser of the 3rd dynasty, addressed to a prince of Elephantine, telling the latter of the king's great anxiety because the Nile had not risen and there had been no inundation for seven years. Unable to account for this, the king had summoned to his presence one of the great wise men, Imhotep, and had questioned him regarding the gods of the Nile who controlled its sources and the inundation. The wise man consulted his books and returned to the king with a report that the god Khnum was the controlling divinity at the cataract whence, according to Egyptian belief, the inundation came. The king, overjoyed, ordered a sacrifice to be offered to the cataract god and that night in a dream Khnum appeared to him and promised to cause the regular and unfailing rise of the Nile thereafter.

This seven years' failure of the Nile occurred probably some 1,200 or 1,300 years before the time of Joseph, but it is interesting to find that such an occurrence was not an impossibility in time long before the Hebrews ever saw Egypt.

(87) Ninety-two foot obelisk still lying in the Assuan granite quarry at the first cataract, Egypt. Copyright 1904 by Underwood & Underwood.

[87] 92 foot obelisk still lying in the Assuan granite quarry at the first cataract

(88) Remarkable inscription of a Seven Years' Famine, on the Island of Sehel (1st cataract)—Egypt. Copyright 1904 by Underwood & Underwood.

[88] Remarkable inscription of a Seven Years' Famine, on the Island of Sehel, first cataract

[89] The building of the great dam across this river will store up an enormous volume of waters at the time of the annual freshets and provide for abundant irrigation of the agricultural districts after the natural subsidence of the river, thus increasing vastly the resources of the country. But an inevitable consequence of the completion of the reservoir will be the rising of the waters around this famous island till only the tops of the taller buildings are left visible.

Set like a peerless gem among the wild, desolate rocks of the cataract, still softened and enriched by the swaying palms in which every Egyptian temple should be framed, this temple and its island have preserved and still awaken more of the romance of the Nile than any other spot in Egypt. We are facing exactly south; behind us are Assuan, Elephantine and the tombs of the frontier nobles. The little square stone building on the right is the house of the custodian of the island. Just in the middle of our prospect you observe the pylons of the temple of Isis. The little building at the left of the temple is the lovely columned kiosk which is so fondly remembered by all Nile travelers. On the left shore you notice a piece of squared masonry which formed part of an ancient quay of the town once occupying the island. There must have been a shrine of Isis on this island long before the present temple was built — but the earliest mention of the place in Egyptian inscriptions is about the middle of the 4th century B.C.

[90] We are at the southwest of the island, looking northeastward across its buildings.

Over on the right is the square kiosk which the natives call "Pharaoh's Bed"; it has no roof and never was finished, but it is one of the gems of the place. It dates back from the Roman age. The building with the large pylon is the Isis temple. That little obelisk is one of a pair — the other has been carried to England. They were erected in the time of Ptolemy IX who died in 117 B.C. and are of especial interest because the one now in England was the monument which enabled Champollion to take the first steps in his decipherment of the hieroglyphic, before he employed the Rosetta stone.

Landing here at the southern end of the court, pilgrims entered between the obelisks and many an imposing procession in honor of the great goddess must have moved up between those colonnades. Isis was the great divinity of the place. The fame of her power had spread far and wide, and in classic times she was worshiped from the Danube and the Seine to the upper cataract of the Nile. Roman ladies journeyed to this shrine to carry home the sacred waters that bathed the island. So powerful was the priesthood of this temple that the edict of Theodosius in 378 A.D., forbidding the continuance of pagan worhsip in the Egyptian temples could not be enforced here and it was not until the reign of Justinian, 527-565 A.D., that the people of this locality ceased to worship the great goddess.

[89]   The templed island of Philae, the "Pearl of Egypt," doomed to destruction

[90]   Looking down upon the island of Philae and its temples from the island of Bigeh

[91] That long, low wall out there means bread for the peasant but destruction to this beautiful monument of his ancestors. Millions of cubic yards of the great life-giving river run to waste in the sea without having benefited the land at all; it is imperative to stop this waste in a practically rainless land hence the barrage below Cairo, the dam at Assiut, and this great barrier which you see yonder, the greatest dam that ever was built. The foundation stone of the vast structure — which is a mile and a quarter long, 100 feet high at the deepest part, and 88 feet thick at the bottom — was laid in 1899 and it was completed in 1902. It is entirely of granite and is controlled by a set of 180 sluices. The water can be raised 65 feet behind it and there is thus collected all around us here a lake containing roughly as much as Geneva Lake in Switzerland. This is then discharged gradually, after the inundation has subsided in Lower Egypt, and it is estimated that not less than $13,000,000 will be added annually to the wealth of Egypt by the recovery of otherwise waste lands.

But, meanwhile, what will become of this beautiful island? Only the tops of these buildings will project from the water, for its surface will rise to the top of that heap of earth on the left. When the addition to the dam — a contemplated increase in the height — is completed, the temples will be largely submerged. It is therefore only a matter of a comparatively short time before this lovely spot will have become a mud-covered, desolate waste.

[92] We stand on the west side of the Nile, looking nearly eastward across the temple of the ancient town of Talmis, now called Kalabsheh. This is Nubia, and the people about us speak the Nubian tongue. As Egyptian civilization gradually spread in the country, the Pharaohs built temples here after the Egyptian style.

The sanctuary before us was built in the days of the Roman Emperor Augustus. We view it from the rear on the high ground of the sandstone bluffs. The front part of the building is wider and higher than the rear, and in the larger section is the hypostyle hall of which you see the roof has now fallen in. In this end of the smaller section is the Holy of Holies. In a chamber on the right of this portion of the building you observe the upper steps of a stairway leading to the roof while at its other end, in perfect preservation and very prominent from here, is a double stairway leading from the lower roof of the chambers in the rear to the higher roof of the hypostyle hall before them.

It is the most picturesque temple in Nubia with the exception of Abu Simbel. With the rough brick huts of the Nubian village grouped closely about it, the background of palms fringing the gleaming river, an idle sail flapping lazily in the light breeze and the sandstone bluffs behind all, it makes a scene pregnant with those melancholy but delightful reveries which only such a ruin in the far East can beget.

(91) The great Assuan Dam, N. W. from the first pylon of the Philae Temple—Egypt. Copyright 1904 by Underwood & Underwood.

[91] The great Assuan Dam, seen from the Philae temple

(92) The Nubian temple of Kalabsheh, built in the days of the Roman Emperor Augustus (view E.)—Egypt. Copyright 1904 by Underwood & Underwood.

[92] The Nubian temple of Kalabsheh, built in the days of the Roman Emperor Augustus

[93] There is the reach of river up which we have come. We are stationed on a lofty, fortified rock on the east bank known as Kasr Ibrim and we look down the river. The river winds through the sandstone table-land with the merest narrow fringe of vegetation demarking it from the desert behind on either hand, and that scanty margin of cultivable land is Nubia, so far as habitable territory is concerned. Wild and hostile tribes have, to be sure, inhabited the desert on either side from time immemorial, but the settled towns have depended solely upon these narrow shores for their sustenance. Away back in the days of Abraham, the Pharaohs made a conquest of this territory between the two cataracts, thus adding over 200 miles of Nile valley to their kingdom. About 1580 B.C. the conquest was gradually pushed further south until the fourth cataract was made the frontier. In the 8th century B.C. this region regained its independence and maintained itself as a separate kingdom far down into the Christian centuries. At this place we are crossing the extremest limits of the vast Roman empire, the other end of which was lost in the forests of the northern British Isles. The Nubians eventually thrust the Romans out of this territory and, having been Christianized from the 4th century on, continued as a Christian power until the conquest of the Moslems in 640 A.D. when Mohammedanism gradually gained the upper hand.

[94] When modern travelers rediscovered Abu Simbel, the descriptions of its glory which reached Europe were considered wild exaggerations. But we have seen how the cliffs in this Nubian country approach often to the very water's edge, leaving the architect no vantage ground for his temples. With what triumphant skill and consummate art he has here overcome this difficulty by hewing this temple out of the solid rock! Seen through the rigging of this feluka the temple does not produce the impression of size of which it is capable. That front is 119 feet wide and over 100 feet high. It is crowned by a cornice of sacred apes, and a niche in the center above the door contains a figure of the god Horus. The four gigantic colossi which adorn the facade are each 65 feet in height, and they, as well as the whole front and the interior chambers, were hewn from the mountain as they stand.

It was wrought by Ramses II, the author of the most colossal works in Egypt. The statues all represent himself and are excellent portraits. Beside them are smaller figures of various members of his family. At the extreme left or south is his daughter Nebet-towe, between the feet of the southernmost colossus an unknown princess, while next to her is another daughter named Bint-Anath. The colossus at the left of the door has unfortunately fallen and the upper portions lie in fragments at its feet. Beside this colossus also are royal ladies of Ramses' family; on the left of the feet is his mother Tuye, and to the right Nofretere, his wife.

(93) Kasr Ibrim (the fort of Ibrim) and a Nile vista to the N. N. E. in lower Nubia, Egypt. Copyright 1904 by Underwood & Underwood.

[93]   Kasr Ibrim and the Nile, lower Nubia

(94) The grotto-temple of Abu Simbel, seen N.W. from a boat on the Nile —Egypt. Copyright 1904 by Underwood & Underwood.

[94]   The grotto temple of Abu Simbel from a boat on the Nile

[95] We have climbed up the side of a steep cliff on the west bank of the Nile and are standing just south of the southernmost of the four colossi; with the river at the right and the cliffs at our left we face northward.

How puny appears the figure of that tall native compared with the gigantic form of the Pharaoh! He is not longer than the beard of the nearer figure. The Pharaoh sits in the ceremonious posture demanded of the divine ruler of the two Egypts, with hands reposing on his knees. He wears the tall double crown symbolic of his double realm of Upper and Lower Egypt. The crown rests upon a headdress of plaited linen. This beard is artificial and was symbolic. Osiris had worn such a beard when he ruled among men. Over the forehead is the sacred uraeus serpent. On the breast under the beard and suspended from the king's neck is a ring bearing his name in hieroglyphics, and here on the right we also read the words, "Beloved of Amon, Usermare-Setepnere," the latter part being the prenomen of Ramses II. The head is beautifully wrought and the expression of the face is one of kindness and benevolence combined with that impressive calm and a subtle touch of oriental indolence mingled with the imperturbability which in both ancient and modern minds are associated with royalty in the East. Can we not easily understand how the Nubians worshiped the Pharaoh, as we look at these giant forms which for over 3,000 years have directed the same impassive gaze over the swift-flowing river toward the rising sun?

[96] We stand here on the sand, which sifts in continually on the north side from the desert behind the cliffs and threatens to engulf the temple. It has been several times cleared away and can be kept out only by the closest vigilance. We look southward across the temple front with the river on our left and the desert on the right. This point shows us, better than any other, the court before the entrance. The face of the cliff has been excavated for some distance in order to obtain the necessary depth for the great statues. All that excavation of the rock, 100 feet high, was done for the most part with bronze chisels. The court is enclosed by a low balustrade running along in front of the statues.

The legs of the further two colossi bear a number of Phoenician, Greek and Carian inscriptions, one of which, on the legs of the fallen colossus, is of great interest being among the oldest known Greek inscriptions. It was placed there by soldiers of King Psamtik, early in the 6th century B.C.

Above the statues is a horizontal line of large hieroglyphics just below the cornice. It contains in duplicate the pompous titulary of Ramses II, the original of the colossal portrait statues. At the top is a line of sacred dog-headed apes crowning the whole. These animals were especially connected with sun-worship and hence we find them here, facing the rising sun, with fore-paws raised in adoration.

(95) The sixty-five foot portrait statues of Ramses II., before rock hewn temple of Abu Simbel, Egypt. Copyright 1904 by Underwood & Underwood.

[95] The 65 foot portrait statues of Ramses II in front of the rock hewn temple of Abu Simbel

(96) 9015 Looking up the river across front of Abu Simbel temple from the sand drift at north. Egypt. Copyright 1904 by Underwood & Underwood.

[96] Looking up river across the front of Abu Simbel temple, from the sand drift at north

[97] We are standing in the entrance door looking westward directly down the main axis of the temple. The river and the rising sun are directly behind us.

At our right and left are the doorposts of the great entrance door, carved with the name of Ramses II as you see most clearly on the left. Beyond the door the great vestibule hall expands before us. It is 54 by 58 feet and the eight massive Osiris pillars which support the roof are 30 feet high. They represent Ramses II in the form of Osiris.

Looking through the door opposite us we see the hypostyle hall — 36 feet wide and 25 feet deep; you observe in the middle one of the hawks, such as we saw outside on the base of the fallen colossus. The door behind the hawk leads to a transverse ante-chamber, beyond which is the Holy of Holies. Through that last door we look into the holy place itself and discern in the dim light the distant figures of two of the four gods who occupy it. These are Amon-Re, the state god, on the left and Ramses II himself on the right. The two others seated there are Ptah of Memphis on the left and Re-Harmachis of Heliopolis on the right, but they are cut off from our view by the doorposts on either side. Thus the gods of the three great religious centers of Egypt — Thebes, Heliopolis and Memphis, are here sacred in this temple in Nubia, and with them is associated the Pharaoh himself, the lord of Nubia. From the threshold on which we stand to that distant rear wall, it is 180 feet — hewn out of solid rock.

[98] This point is nearly 1,000 miles from Alexandria and the sea. Our point of view is on the west beside an elevated rock known as Abusir. We look northeastward down the rocky gorge, over the wild prospect of the cataract. It is now March and the waters have been falling for four or five months; but, in the time of the inundation, it is an impressive sight to see the river rushing over these stubborn rocks which for ages have resisted the erosion of the stream. They are chiefly granite, with outcroppings of other similar rocks which break up the stream into numerous tortuous channels, or when submerged, harass the waters into a wild and fearful tumult of successive leaps and plunges, churning the flood for miles into a boiling cauldron flecked with yellow foam. This was the frontier of the Middle Kingdom whose kings first made conquest of lower Nubia, although to maintain it they built a series of forts in the valley or on the islands in the stream for 30 miles above this point. The tribes which they kept in subjection 4,000 years ago had not in the year of grace 1883 yet lost their aggressiveness, for at that time, under their skillful leader the Mahdi, they regained their independence and eventually drove back the British to this cataract. The frontier post of the British then became Wadi Halfa, about 5 miles down stream directly on our present line of sight on the other side of the river. That is, the frontier became essentially the same as that of the Pharaohs in the days of Abraham. There it remained until the British in 1896-7 pushed a railway from Wadi Halfa out into the desert on our right.

[97] Interior of the rock hewn temple of Abu Simbel

[98] Second cataract of the Nile, the first obstruction to navigation for 1,000 miles

[99] Omdurman is on the left bank of the White Nile, just where the Blue Nile flows into it. As we stand now both rivers are on our right but out of range. We face northeast, that is, down stream; Khartum is also on our right but out of range on the south bank of the Blue Nile. When General "Chinese" Gordon entered Khartum in 1884 in the endeavor to save the Sudan from the Mahdi, he rode to his death and the small body of troops sent for his relief, which nearly a year later succeeded in forcing their way into Khartum under General Sir Charles Wilson, found that the town had fallen but two days before and that Gordon had perished. It was not until 1896 that, beginning the construction of the railway through the desert from Wadi Halfa, the Egyptians under British officers and with a nucleus of British regulars, advanced for the recovery of the Sudan and the upper river. On September 2, 1898, Sir Herbert Kitchener, out on the slopes of the Kerreri Hills which you see at the left, fought a decisive battle with the dervishes; Kitchener entered the town here on the afternoon of the same day when the native Egyptian troops, although themselves Mohammedans, blew up the tomb before us and thus prevented it from becoming a shrine to which the dervishes were beginning to make pilgrimages. Such pilgrimages might have resulted in religious uprisings like that of the once potent Mahdi.

The tomb is, as you see, a low, roofless building with arched windows, surrounded by a court with an arched door on the right. The low roof on the right beyond the court is the Mahdi's house.

[100] There is no point at the new Egyptian capital of the Sudan where a better idea of the life and character of the place could be obtained than just where we are now standing. We look a little south of westward across the Blue Nile and the city of Khartum on the opposite side of the river. The town was founded by Mohammed Ali in 1823 and soon became a flourishing trade center for the products of the Sudan. Out there on the left of this first smokestack is the palace in which the governor of the Sudan lives. It is built on the spot where Gordon fell.

This boat nearest us is taking on a body of troops for transport to Fashoda, 510 miles further up the White Nile. This service involves danger and the steamer is armored for its work. But the boats, though prepared for war, are messengers of civilization, penetrating to the heart of Africa. Possibly the adventurous nobles of Elephantine, whose tombs we visited there, had already penetrated in their trading expeditions to this junction of the two rivers, but the country above has always lain in complete darkness. The remotest monuments of ancient Egypt are over 400 miles below us here and the Pharaohs never dominated the country on either side of this Blue Nile.

(99) 8610 Tomb of the Mahdi at Omdurman—Kerreri hills at left, scene of Kitchener's victory—Sudan. Copyright 1904 by Underwood & Underwood.

[99] The tomb of the Mahdi at Omdurman with the Kerreri hills at left, Sudan

(100) Governor's Palace, and armored steamer leaving Khartum for Fashoda and the Blue Nile, Sudan. Copyright 1904 by Underwood & Underwood.

[100] Governor's palace, and armored steamer leaving Khartum for Fashoda and the Blue Nile, Sudan

FAREWELL

And so we take final leave of this remarkable river and the valley which it wrought, as a cradle of early civilization. Civilization has always moved up river valleys, and we have together journeyed in the footprints of early man as he passed up this, the most interesting valley in the orient where any remains of early man are found. We have seen his traces gradually disappear, until at this point we stand on the verge of the great uncivilized heart of Africa, from which the river issues. Equally primitive must once have been the life of the men of the lower Nile, and, as we have moved up the river we have thus followed the stream of civilization from its later and more developed phases to its modern primitive survivals in the Sudan. Not that the Sudan is the source of Egyptian civilization, but it is today in much the same material condition in which the trading nobles of Elephantine must have found it nearly 5,000 years ago.

James Henry Breasted,
April 1, 1905